# First Steps
# With
# Your Computer

## Tom Mac Mahon

Blackrock Education Centre
2006

3465813

Blackrock Education Centre
Kill Avenue, Dún Laoghaire
Co. Dublin, Ireland

Tel. (+3531) 2302709    Fax. (+3531) 2365044
Email. sales@blackrockec.ie    Web. www.becpublishing.com

First Published 2006

ISBN 0954790111

*For Máire, Helen and Joan*

# Production Team

*Author*
Tom Mac Mahon

*Editor*
Richard Butler

*Design and Layout*
Annette Bolger

*Illustrations*
Pollie Venn

*Proofreader*
Claire Rourke

*Cover Design*
Vermillion

*Acknowledgements*

Thanks are due to many people who made this book possible. I would like in particular to acknowledge the invaluable assistance of the following:

The members of the Blackrock, Foxrock, Johnstown/Killiney and Dún Laoghaire Active Retired Associations' computer classes, whose experiences and requirements initiated the project, and the Dún Laoghaire VEC Adult Education Service which facilitated it.

Sister Pauline and the members of the adult beginners computer classes at the Warrenmount Centre who all provided further insights into what beginners actually need and enjoy.

All my second-language English students over the years who taught me how to avoid jargon and explain things as simply as possible.

Carrie Fonseca and Emer Bradley at BEC for all their help and encouragement.

Deirdre Keyes of Dún Laoghaire VEC for her valuable assistance.

Annette Bolger for her patience.

Special thanks to Patrick Harrington for a titular suggestion.

*Tom MacMahon*
*March 2006*

# Contents

# Start Here

This book was written following a series of classes given by the author to people who had never used a computer before. Their needs and experiences form the basis of the book.

It will guide *you* in your first steps with your new computer.

Explanations are in simple English without jargon.

Chapters are short and deal with only one thing at a time.

Illustrations show you, as far as possible, exactly what you will see on your computer screen.

Step-by-step instructions make everything easy to follow and understand.

Using this book, you will learn how to:

- **Use the computer** and the **mouse**,

- **Write a letter** or document and print it out,

- **Send email** to your friends and relations,

- **Receive email** and reply to email messages,

- **Use the Internet** for information and entertainment,

- **Play a music CD** or a **video DVD**... and more.

Why should you put off learning how to use a computer, now that they are to be found in practically every home and office?

This book will help you to break the ice!
# Using the Book

**Before** you sit down at the computer, **Chapter 1** tells you about the different parts of the computer and what they are used for. You will also learn how to turn the computer on and off. **Chapter 2** tells you about the mouse and how it is used to control the computer.

**Sitting at the computer, Chapters 3** to **6** use programs already on the computer to teach you how to use the mouse. You will learn how to use the computer – without stress and in your own time. **Chapter 7** tells you about the keyboard and some commonly used keys.

**Using the skills** you have learnt in the earlier chapters, **Chapter 8 onwards** shows you how to write a letter, send and receive email and how to use the Internet. You will soon be able to use the computer for interest and enjoyment.

You will learn how to save letters and documents. You will learn how to find them again later and how to edit or change them, if you need to.

You will learn how to use your computer to play a music CD while you work. You will learn how to watch a DVD film on your computer, if your computer has a DVD player installed.

A final chapter gives you advice on buying a computer. It tells you what you should look for and helps you to make a decision about the various options that may be available.

# CHAPTER 1
# The Computer

This chapter describes the computer
and what it can be used for.
You will learn about the different
parts of a computer and what they
are for.

# The Computer

A computer is just a machine like any other. You can learn to use a computer just as you can learn to use any other machine. However, there are some people who regard computers as being 'difficult'. Perhaps this is because many people try to use a computer with little or no instruction on how to use it. Hence the fear and alarm when something unexpected happens and they do not know what to do.

But now that computers are so widely used, both in the home and in the workplace, why not learn a little about them?

If you see the computer for what it is and take a little time to learn how to use it, your interests can be enriched and your work reduced… and it can be a fulfilling and happy experience.

## ARE COMPUTERS EASY TO USE?

Yes. When you have learnt the basic skills – and they really are basic – modern computers **are** easy to use. Long ago, however, computers **were** very difficult for ordinary people to use. All that appeared on the screen then was text – and only text. Instructions had to be typed in using the keyboard in a special code to get the computer to do anything.

The Computer

3

1

In 1984, Apple introduced the Macintosh computer and described it as 'the computer for the rest of us'.

It used little pictures, called **icons**, on the screen to represent documents and programs. It used a small rolling box, called a **mouse**, to control the computer.

Icons on the computer screen

The Macintosh quickly became very popular and successful because 'ordinary people' found that they could use it without having to be 'computer experts'.

Other computer makers soon followed suit, notably with the introduction of the similar 'Windows' system on their computers.

### One Thing at a Time

A computer is really many different machines in one.

A music system in your living room, for example, can play CDs, cassettes and also receive radio programmes. You learn how to use each part separately.

Pressing the wrong button could interrupt an interesting radio programme and start playing a CD instead. Most of us can quickly correct the situation but, when something similar happens on a computer, panic sets in!

Learn to do one thing at a time with your new computer and you will soon become familiar with it.

The Computer

1

First, there are the simple things, such as **turning the computer on** and **off**.

Then you will need to **understand what you see** on the screen and know what all the little pictures – or icons – represent.

You will need to learn how to   to get the computer to do what you want it to do.

You must learn **to read**, and know how **to respond** to, messages that may pop up on the screen now and again.

While you can do many things with the computer using just the mouse, you will also need to use the **keyboard** from time to time. You do not have to become an expert typist but, if you want to send email messages to your friends or prepare letters or other documents, learning to use the keyboard properly is an advantage. The computer can be a typing tutor and teach you to type at your own pace!

## WHAT ARE COMPUTERS USED FOR?

For many users, the computer replaces the typewriter. People everywhere use computers to prepare letters and documents of all kinds.

The letters and documents can be **stored** on the computer and they can be **reused** or **modified** for any particular use or occasion without having to be typed out all over again.

Individually addressed letters can be sent to different people without the need to type more than one copy of the letter or any of the addresses more than once.

Increasingly, people now use their computers to **send and receive email** instead of writing and posting letters.

The Computer

1

Email is delivered nearly instantaneously worldwide at almost no cost.

Computer programs for learning and enjoyment are available at all levels and in all subjects depending on what you want to achieve.

## WHAT CAN COMPUTERS DO?

In school or business, the computer has endless uses. It can keep track of employee or pupil records. It can prepare lists and keep accounts. It can be used to produce drawings. It can generally make the production of every kind of document a simple matter, and enable the user to produce it to a very high standard.

Here are just a very few of the things the computer can help you to do at home.

Listen to **music** on your computer, even while you are using it to do something else at the same time.

Watch **films** with a picture quality that is better than television.

Have instant **email** contact with people at home or overseas.

See **information** on every conceivable subject on the Internet.

The Computer

1

6

Search for the cheapest **holiday flights** and book them from your home.

But you do not have to learn to do everything at once. If you take one thing at a time, you will find that the computer is not something to be afraid of. Instead, you will find that it is a machine that can lighten your daily tasks and assist with your hobbies and interests.

## THE PARTS OF A COMPUTER

A computer is usually supplied as a set of different parts that have to be connected together before it can be used. Typically, these are a large box that contains the 'brains' of the computer, the screen, also known as the **monitor**, the **mouse**, **keyboard**, **loudspeakers** and an assortment of **cables** to connect them all together and plug in to the mains.

### The Computer 'Box'

The main box is called the **Central Processing Unit**, or **CPU** for short.

All the other bits and pieces connected to the CPU box are to enable you to use what the box contains.

These are the principal things in the box.

The **Motherboard** is the main electronic circuit board of the computer. It has lots of **chips** and other items on it which do all the work.

The **Hard Disk** is a sealed box containing a metal magnetic disk on which information is recorded – stored – just as music or video is recorded on magnetic tape.

The Computer

1

The **Programs** that the computer uses to operate and the work you produce on the computer are all stored on the Hard Disk so that you can use them again the next time you switch the computer on.

The **CD** and/or **DVD** drive is a unit containing a mechanism for using CD and/or DVD disks. CD or DVD disks can contain music, video or computer programs.

The **Floppy Disk** drive is a unit containing a mechanism for using floppy disks. A floppy disk consists of a soft flexible plastic disk in a hard protective plastic container (many modern computers do not come with these supplied).

Floppy disks are used to transfer information between computers or to send to other people.

The **Power Supply** unit is used to obtain suitable power from the mains supply for everything in the box.

### The Monitor

The computer screen – known as the **monitor** – was often the largest, bulkiest and heaviest part of the computer. Lighter and more compact flat screens are now mostly used instead.

Its purpose is to show – or monitor – what is happening inside the main computer box.

The monitor translates the internal, and invisible, electronic workings of the computer into pictures on its screen that people can recognise and work with.

An important part of learning to use a computer is learning to understand what you see displayed on the monitor.

The Computer

1

## The Mouse

The **mouse** is used to control the computer, to tell it what to do. It is held gently in the hand and moved around on a little mat beside the keyboard.

The movement and position of the mouse is duplicated exactly by a small **Cursor**, or **Pointer**, on the screen.

A mouse usually has two **buttons** that can be pressed to send further instructions to the computer.

The mouse is used for almost everything – to open a program, select text, and so on.

## The Keyboard

The **keyboard** is necessary for preparing all kinds of documents. It has the same layout as a typewriter keyboard but there are a number of extra keys for use with the computer.

There is usually a set of number keys on the right, calculator style. You can use these number keys if you are dealing with a lot of figures and find them more convenient than using the number keys along the top of the keyboard.

The Computer

1

9

### The Loudspeakers

Two small **loudspeakers** are usually supplied separately but some computers may have them built into the monitor. The loudspeakers can play various sounds to let you know when the computer is doing something and wants to let you know.

### Turning On the Computer

A **button**, usually on the front of the main computer box, is pressed to turn on the computer.

The monitor must also be turned on. There is usually a button on the front.

The loudspeakers may also need to be turned on separately.

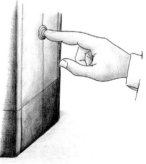

After turning on, it takes a few moments for the computer to start up.

While the computer is starting up, you may see various messages, which can be ignored.

When the computer has finished starting up, a musical chime may be heard and the main display appears.

You will recognise the main display by the appearance of the **Start** button in the bottom left-hand corner of the screen.

You are then ready to start using the computer.

The Computer

1

## Turning Off the Computer

Most people use the mouse to click 'buttons' on the screen (you will learn how to do this later).

This is what happens.

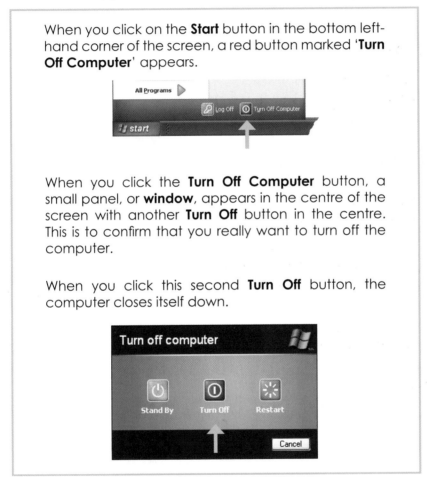

When you click on the **Start** button in the bottom left-hand corner of the screen, a red button marked '**Turn Off Computer**' appears.

When you click the **Turn Off Computer** button, a small panel, or **window**, appears in the centre of the screen with another **Turn Off** button in the centre. This is to confirm that you really want to turn off the computer.

When you click this second **Turn Off** button, the computer closes itself down.

Many people also turn off the monitor every time they turn off the computer but this is not strictly necessary.

The Computer

1

Modern computers using Windows XP can also be turned off by pressing the same button on the front of the CPU box that you used to turn it on. The computer then first checks that everything is in order before it actually turns itself off.

## IMPORTANT!

Do **not** turn off the computer by turning off the switch on the wall socket.

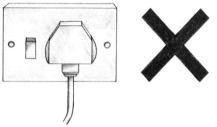

If you turn off the power at the wall, the computer does not get a chance to check that everything is in order before it closes down. This may cause problems the next time you switch it on again.

The Computer

1

## In this chapter, you have learnt...

- about the different parts of a computer.

- some of the things you can do with a computer.

- how to turn the computer on.

- how to turn the computer off.

## Do you remember...

- where the 'brains' of the computer are?

- what the monitor shows you?

- what the hard disk is used for?

- what floppy disks are used for?

The Computer

1

# CHAPTER 2
# The Mouse

This chapter tells you more about the mouse.
It describes how it works and how to use it.

# The Mouse

Before you turn on your computer, take a little time to read through this chapter. The mouse was introduced to help people use computers more easily than had been the case previously. It is called a mouse because of its mouse-like shape. The cable that connects the box to the computer is like a mouse's tail.

Using the mouse with **confidence** and **ease** is the **key** to using the computer effectively.

## HOW DOES IT WORK?

The most commonly used mouse has a ball protruding through a hole on the underside. As you move the mouse on a surface, the ball rotates and sends details of its movements to the computer. It works best when the mouse is on a special pad called a **mouse mat**.

An **optical mouse** uses a light beam to sense movement instead of a rolling ball.

A **wireless mouse** does not need a cable to connect it to the computer.

The Mouse

2

Moving the mouse over the mat causes a **cursor**, or **pointer**, to move in exactly the same way on the computer screen.

The mouse thus converts the movement of your hand into a similar movement of the cursor on the screen.

## MOUSE BUTTONS

Most mice have two buttons. They are each used for different purposes. The left-hand button is the one most often used while the right-hand button is used for less frequent actions.

> If you are **left-handed**, the actions performed by the buttons can be swapped over to suit you (see Appendix, page 289).

By pressing a button, you give an instruction to the computer to perform an action.

Co-ordinating the movement of your hand (on the mouse), your finger (on the button) and your eye (on the screen) may be difficult at first but it becomes second nature with a little practice.

## HOLDING THE MOUSE

Grip the mouse firmly, but gently, between the thumb on the one side and the fingers on the other, leaving the index finger free to press the buttons. Then move it over the mouse mat, holding it all the time.

Do not push it around with your open palm without gripping it. It will not respond exactly as you intended and neither will the computer.

The Mouse

2

The mouse's tail must also point straight ahead – **away from you**. If you turn the mouse sideways while you are using it, the pointer on the screen will not match your movements and both you and the computer will be confused.

You should move the mouse around **gently** on the mouse mat. You do not have to press it down. Press the buttons gently. Pressing the buttons very hard will make no difference to the computer apart from placing extra strain and wear on them – and on you.

## THE MOUSE MAT

A little problem that you will encounter very quickly is that you will sometimes reach the edge of the mouse mat before the pointer on the screen has got to where you want it to go. What do you do then?

The answer is to lift the mouse up off the mat so that it loses contact with it. Then place the mouse back down again in the centre of the mat.

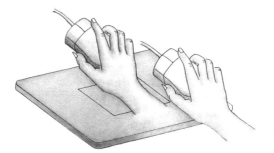

The Mouse

2

While the mouse is **off the mat**, the pointer on the screen stays where it is and does not move.

When you return the mouse to the **centre of the mouse mat**, the pointer moves again – as you move the mouse – to complete your original intention.

## USING THE MOUSE

The mouse is deceptively simple to use but it will require some practice before it can be used with ease and confidence.

Using the mouse automatically is **the key to confidence** in using the computer. The chapters that follow use programs already on your computer to give you plenty of practice with the mouse before you even think of using the keyboard.

The mouse is used for three different things – **pointing**, **clicking** and **dragging**.

It is most important to know the difference between these different actions. Then you will be able to use the one appropriate to what you want to do, without having to think about it.

### Pointing

Pointing means moving the **pointer**, usually in the shape of a small arrowhead, on the screen so that the sensitive part – the **tip** of the arrow – rests on an object on the screen.

As you move the mouse, the pointer on the screen moves with it. You can point to anything on the screen quickly and easily just by moving the mouse.

To **point** to something on the screen, move the mouse until the **tip** of the arrow **rests** on the object.

The Mouse

2

By pointing to an object, you are selecting it from all the other available objects for a particular purpose.

Pointing does **not** mean placing the arrow **near** the object or **beside** the object or some distance from it. The **tip** of the arrowhead must rest **on** and **inside** the object.

Remember, it is only the very **tip** of the pointer that is sensitive. It is the tip that must be **inside** the object. Otherwise the computer will think that you are pointing to something else.

## Clicking

**Clicking** means pressing and **quickly** releasing one of the buttons on the mouse. Pressing and releasing the button produces an audible 'click' from the mouse to let you know that you have performed the action.

You must **hold the mouse still** when you are clicking.

If the mouse moves, even slightly, while you are clicking, the pointer may move away from the object. The computer then thinks that you are pointing to something else and it will respond differently.

When you have pointed to an object, clicking will then tell the computer to perform an action related to that object.

Most clicking is done with the **left** button.

If you are asked to click with the **right** button, the term **right-click** is used.

## How Many Clicks?

A single click tells the computer to do something. The click must be done quickly – by pressing and releasing the button without a pause – or the computer will think that you are **holding down** the button before you release it. Then it will not recognise your action as a click and you will wonder why nothing happened!

The Mouse

2

21

Two clicks in quick succession, called **double clicking**, are commonly used for certain purposes. The second click must follow without a pause or the computer will interpret them as two separate single clicks.

## Dragging

**Dragging** means **pressing** and **holding down** a mouse button, then **moving** the mouse before releasing the button. Dragging is used to move an object from one part of the screen to another or to select text in a document, just two examples that you will use later.

This is how to move an object on the screen.

First **point** to the object on the screen.

This means placing the **tip** of the pointer inside the object (not near it or beside it).

Then **press** and **hold down** the button while you move the mouse on its mat. The object on the screen follows your movement.

Release the button.

This is how to select a piece of text.

First **point** to either the beginning or the end of the piece of text you want to select.

Then, **holding down** the button, move to the other end of the piece of text.

Release the button. The selected text now appears with a band of colour through it as if you had used a highlighter.

The Mouse

2

In this chapter, you have learnt...

- how the mouse works.

- about the mouse buttons.

- how to hold the mouse.

- how to return the mouse from the edge to the centre of the mouse mat.

Do you remember...

- how to point?

- how to click?

- how to drag?

- which button is used most?

The Mouse

2

## CHAPTER 3
# Using the Mouse

This chapter gives you practice in using the mouse.
You will use a calculator and play a card game on the computer.

# Using the Mouse

Now, with your computer switched on (see Chapter 1; page 10), you are ready to practise what you have been reading about the mouse.

Note that you must **not** hold the mouse at an angle or sideways. If you do not hold the mouse correctly, the pointer on the screen will **not** move in the same direction as the mouse on the mouse mat.

## POINTING

Move the mouse to do the following and watch the pointer on the screen at the same time.

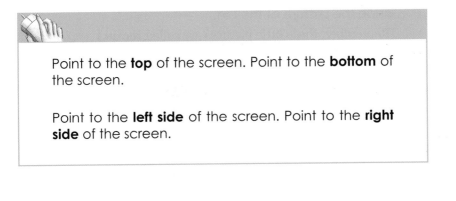

Point to the **top** of the screen. Point to the **bottom** of the screen.

Point to the **left side** of the screen. Point to the **right side** of the screen.

Think of the mouse mat as if it were the screen lying flat on the desk. As you move the mouse over the mouse mat, notice that the pointer moves in exactly the same way over the screen.

Remember that you can pick up the mouse and place it back in the centre of the mouse mat if you go over the edge of the mouse mat.

Move **diagonally** between opposite corners of the screen.

Move in a straight line **up and down** without moving to the left or right.

Move in a straight line to the **left and right** without moving up or down.

Moving left and right without going up or down will be very important later when you are using menus or selecting a line of text in a document.

Point to the **Recycle Bin.**

Make sure that the **sharp tip** of the pointer is actually inside the picture of the bin.
(Remember, these little pictures are called **icons**.)

Point to the centre of the screen.

Point to the **Start** button.

Point to any other icons on the screen.

Point to a blank area of the screen.

You will notice that, apart from the pointer resting where you want it to, nothing else happens. This is because the purpose of pointing is to place the pointer where you want it to be **before** you ask the computer to do something else by clicking or dragging, as you will learn.

## CLICKING

Most clicking is done with the left button. To click, press and release the button once, quickly but gently. You will hear a 'click' sound from the mouse.

If the right button is to be used, you will be asked to **right-click**.

Remember, before you can click on something, you must first **point** to it.

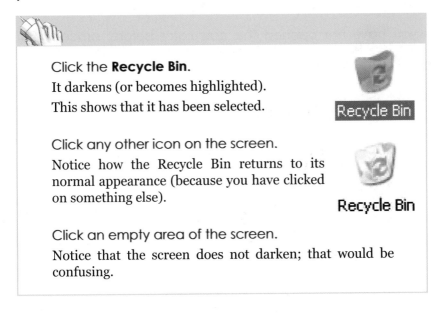

Click the **Recycle Bin**.
It darkens (or becomes highlighted).
This shows that it has been selected.

Recycle Bin

Click any other icon on the screen.
Notice how the Recycle Bin returns to its normal appearance (because you have clicked on something else).

Recycle Bin

Click an empty area of the screen.
Notice that the screen does not darken; that would be confusing.

Using The Mouse

3

Clicking on an object once **selects** it. You are telling the computer that you intend to do something with it.

Only click once on any item just now. If you click more than once, that will tell the computer to do something else, which we do not want to do just yet.

## THE CALCULATOR

In the next few sections, you will practise pointing and clicking. First, you will use the mouse to display a **Calculator** on the screen. Then you will use the Calculator – by pointing and clicking with the mouse – to make some simple calculations.

### Finding the Calculator

If you have not opened the calculator before, proceed as follows. (If you get lost at any point, don't worry. Go back to the **Start** button and begin again.)

Click the green **Start** button (at the bottom left of the screen).

The Start **menu** appears. (See illustration on page 32).

Note that the items in the Start menu vary from computer to computer and may differ from those shown here.

Point to **All Programs** at the bottom of the **Start** menu, just above the Start button (move the mouse until the tip of the pointer is on **All Programs**).

All Programs is highlighted by a band of colour and a new menu appears.

Move the mouse so that the pointer moves across into the new menu. You must move across without going up or down.

Point to **Accessories**, near the top. Accessories is now highlighted and a further menu appears.

Move across into the new menu, without going up or down.

Point to **Calculator** in the new menu (it is near the middle of the menu).
It is now highlighted with a band of colour, as before.

Hold the mouse steady and click on **Calculator** (anywhere on the band of colour will do).
The menus disappear and the calculator appears on the screen.

Congratulations! You have performed a fairly complicated series of actions with the mouse.

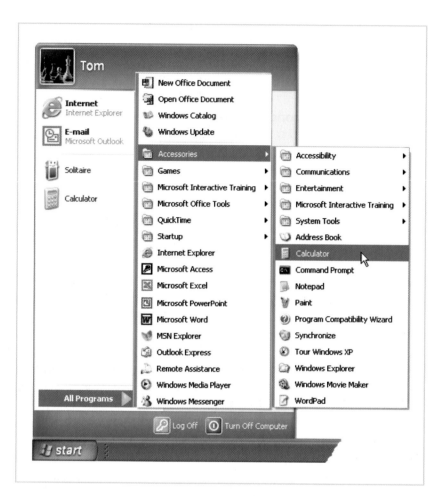

## Using the Calculator

The calculator on the screen works like a real calculator. It is just that you have to use the mouse on the mouse mat to press the buttons on the screen with the pointer.

To press a button on the **Calculator**, point to the button on the **screen** and then click the **mouse button**. The number you click appears in the display panel on the screen calculator, just as it would appear on a calculator on your desk.

Now spend some time clicking the buttons to perform some calculations.

Note that although the computer uses **+** and **-** for addition and subtraction, it uses an asterisk (*) for multiplication and a forward slash (/) for division.

So, instead of looking for the **x** button for multiplication, you must press the asterisk button.

Instead of looking for the ÷ button you must press the forward slash button.

To clear the numbers already on the display, click the button marked **C**.

Using The Mouse

3

## Making Calculations

Try the following.

Remember to click the **=** button to display the answer.

**4 + 16**          **240 – 40**          **45 x 124**          **75 ÷ 3**

**Find percentages:** What is 20 per cent of 45?

First click the **C** button to reset the calculator.

Click **45 x 20**. Then click the **%** button. Did you get the answer **9**?

Click the **C** button again before you do another percentage calculation.

**Find square roots:** What is the square root of 2?

Click **2**. Then click the **sqrt** button. Did you get the answer **1.41421...**?

# DRAGGING

Would you like to move the calculator to a more convenient part of the screen?

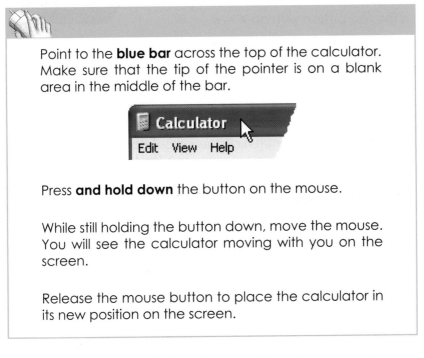

Point to the **blue bar** across the top of the calculator. Make sure that the tip of the pointer is on a blank area in the middle of the bar.

Press **and hold down** the button on the mouse.

While still holding the button down, move the mouse. You will see the calculator moving with you on the screen.

Release the mouse button to place the calculator in its new position on the screen.

Practise moving the **Calculator** to different parts of the screen.

You might also like to practise moving other items on the screen, such as the **Recycle Bin**.

Recycle Bin

However, depending on how your computer is set up, those items may not remain in the position they are dragged to and may return to their original positions.

Using The Mouse

3

## Closing the Calculator

To close the calculator when you are finished and to remove it from the screen, click the **Close** button in the top right-hand corner of the calculator.

It is the red button with an **X** in it.

## Reopening the Calculator

Remember when you opened the calculator for the first time? You had to go through several menus to find it.

The next time you want to use the calculator, you will find it on the **Start** menu as soon as you click the **Start** button.

This is because the computer remembers the most recent programs you use to make it easier for you to find them again.

(Your computer may have several other items in the **Start** menu as well as those shown above.)

Point to the **Calculator** and click anywhere in the band of colour when it is highlighted. It opens. Easy!

Now, why not drag the calculator to the centre of the screen before you begin?

Have another practice with the calculator, and then be ready to try your hand at cards!

## SOLITAIRE

A good way to practise using the mouse is to play the card game **Solitaire** (also widely known as **Patience**) on the computer. The object of the game is to move the cards around to arrange them in order of each of the four suites: Hearts, Diamonds, Spades and Clubs. You do this by **pointing**, **clicking** and **dragging**.

In the game, some of the playing cards in the pack are laid out in little groups across the screen, face down, with the topmost card face up.

The remaining cards are placed face down in a stack in the top left-hand corner.

The illustration on the next page shows a game in progress.

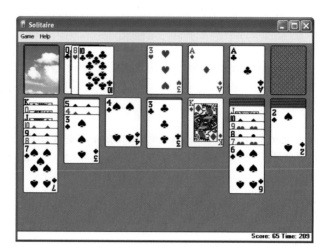

Before you actually open **Solitaire**, the next few sections explain how the game is played.

### Playing the Game

Begin the game by dragging a card at a time – when you can – to arrange the cards in **descending** order in their various groups: **King**, **Queen**, **Jack**, **10**, **9**, **8**, and so on.

However, as you place the cards in order, you cannot have two cards of the same colour together. Thus a **black 7** is placed over a **red 8**, for example, or a **red 7** over a **black 8** (see the illustration above). If you drag a card to a position not allowed by the rules, it will jump back to its original place when you release the mouse button.

### Continue

When the top card of a group has been moved, click the back of the uncovered card to turn it over. Then you can move it to a new position, if there is a place for it.

When no further cards can be moved from group to group, click the pack in the top left-hand corner to display new cards.

Then move the topmost new card, if possible, and so on.

An entire set of face-up cards can be moved from one group to another by dragging the topmost card.

In the game in the illustration, a set whose top card is a **black 8** is being dragged from a group on the right onto a **red 9** in the group on the very left. Then the back of the newly revealed card will be clicked to turn it over and continue the game.

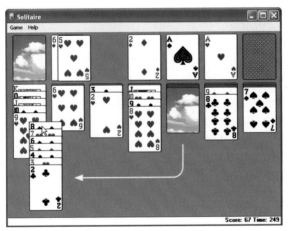

## Places and Aces

If a group place becomes vacant – all its cards having been moved to other groups – a **King** can be placed in the vacant space to start another group. Cards from another group that has a King at the top can also be dragged there.

When an **Ace** appears, drag it to one of the four empty boxes at the top of the screen.

Using The Mouse

3

Then cards of the same colour may be dragged onto the aces in **ascending** order – **Ace**, **1**, **2**, **3**, **4**, and so on – until the four suites are complete.

If you can complete all the suites like this, the game has been completely worked out.

Don't be disappointed if all possibilities run out and you cannot complete the game. Look at the row of F keys (**F1**, **F2**, **F3**...) on the top row on the keyboard.

While you are playing Solitaire, press the **F2** key to start a new game at any time.

## OPENING SOLITAIRE

Now you are ready to open **Solitaire** for the first time. Begin at the **Start** button and go from menu to menu to find it and open it, just as you opened the **Calculator**.

Proceed as follows.

Click the **Start** button.
The Start menu appears.

Point to **All Programs**.

The All Programs menu appears.

Move straight across (try not to go up or down) to the All Programs menu and point to **Games**.

Games is highlighted and the Games menu appears.

Move straight across to the Games menu.

Point to **Solitaire** and then click on it.

The menus disappear and the Solitaire game appears.

Drag **Solitaire** to the centre of the screen. (Point to a blank part of the blue bar at the top. Hold down the mouse button and drag. Then release the button.)

Using The Mouse

3

## Playing Solitaire

When you open **Solitaire**, the cards are dealt for a game as described on the previous pages.

To play the game, **point**, **click** and **drag** with the mouse to move the cards according to the rules outlined on the previous pages.

But be warned, playing **Solitaire** can be addictive!

## Closing Solitaire

Close **Solitaire** in the same way as you closed the Calculator.

Click the red **Close** button in the top right-hand corner of the Solitaire game window.

## Reopening Solitaire

Just like the calculator, you will find **Solitaire** in the **Start** menu the next time you want to play.

Click the **Start** button.

Point to **Solitaire**.
Solitaire is highlighted.

Click anywhere in the band of colour.

Drag **Solitaire** to the centre of the screen, as you did with the calculator, before you begin to play.

## GETTING HELP

Help and other information is often available on the screen.

Open Solitaire, if it is not already open, and proceed as follows.

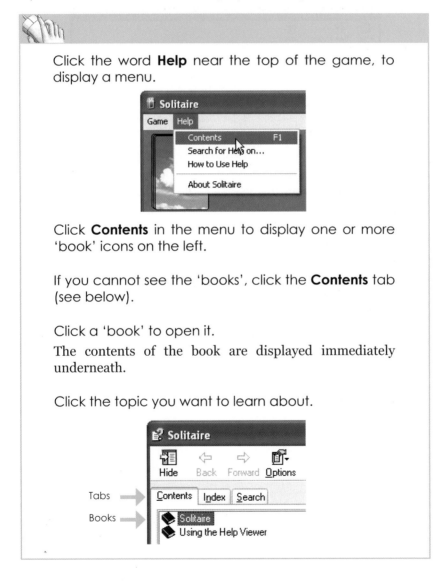

Click the word **Help** near the top of the game, to display a menu.

Click **Contents** in the menu to display one or more 'book' icons on the left.

If you cannot see the 'books', click the **Contents** tab (see below).

Click a 'book' to open it.
The contents of the book are displayed immediately underneath.

Click the topic you want to learn about.

3

Notice that, as you click, the pointer becomes a hand with a pointing finger. (As you use the computer, the pointer changes shape according to what it is being used for.)

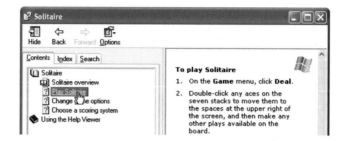

The topic that you clicked appears on the right.

You may see **Related Topics** under the main topic on the right.

Click on **Related Topics**, if you wish, to display more topics to explore.

## The Help Index

The **Help Index** enables you to find help on a specific topic.

Click on the **Index** tab, over the 'books', to display a list of items.

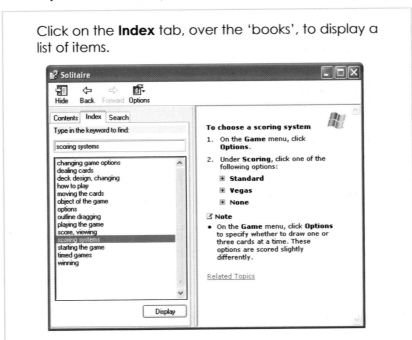

Click an item in the list.

Then click the **Display** button under the list to display that item in full.

To return to the previous display, click the **Back** button just above the **Index** tab.

Click the **Forward** button – to the right of the Back button – to go forward again.

Remember that a **Help** menu is available for almost everything you will do on the computer.

Using The Mouse

45

3

### Closing

If you have opened **Help**, there will be two things on the screen, the **Help** items and the **Game** itself.

The Help items may be on top of the game, or you might have dragged it to one side if it obscured the game.

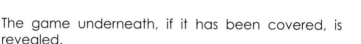

To close **Help** when you are finished, click the red **Close** button in the top right-hand corner of the Help items. It is the button with the **X** in it.

The game underneath, if it has been covered, is revealed.

To close the game, click the red **Close** button in the top right-hand corner of the game.

## TURNING OFF THE COMPUTER

If you want to turn off the computer now, see Chapter 1, page 11 to remind you what to do.

## In this chapter, you have...

- opened, closed and reopened the calculator and Solitaire.

- practised pointing, clicking and dragging with the mouse.

- learnt to find a recently used item in the Start menu.

- learnt how to get Help when you need assistance.

## Do you remember...

- how to find and open the calculator?

- how to find and open Solitaire?

- how to drag the calculator or Solitaire to the centre of the screen?

Using The Mouse

3

## CHAPTER 4
# The Desktop and Windows

This chapter tells you about the computer desktop and what appears on it.
You will also learn about windows and how to use them.

# The Desktop

Everything you have done so far happened on the main screen, which is also known as the **Desktop**.

## WHAT IS THE DESKTOP?

The **Desktop** is the screen that appears when the computer has finished starting up. It is the electronic equivalent of a real desktop.

You can move items around and arrange them on the computer desktop with the mouse, as you have already done with the **Calculator** and with the cards in **Solitaire**.

You should always relate what you are doing on the computer to what you would do on a real desk. This is the secret of working with the computer.

**The Desktop and Windows**

The only difference is that in real life you are working with actual objects on a real desk. With the computer you are working with **pictures** (icons) of those objects on the computer screen.

In both cases you are doing exactly the same thing, whether it is using a calculator, playing a game of cards, painting a picture or writing a letter.

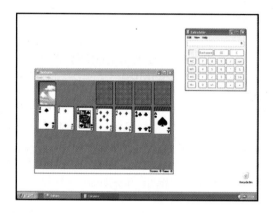

## A Tidy Desktop

Ideally you should keep your computer desktop tidy just as you would keep a real desktop tidy.

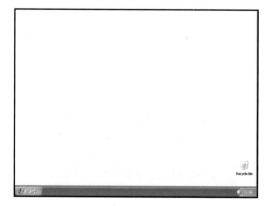

4

When you learn about filing later, you will know how to keep your own desktop tidy.

Notice that there is a bar, called the **Taskbar**, across the bottom of the desktop.

## THE TASKBAR

The **Taskbar** is used to display frequently used items in a convenient way. You have already used the **Start** button on the left-hand end of the taskbar. Clicking the Start button displays the Start menu – the main contents list of what is in the computer. You have already used the **Start button** and the **Start menu** to open various items, such as the Calculator and Solitaire.

Start Button          Open items                                    The time etc.

The **time** is displayed on the right-hand end of the Taskbar. The computer has its own clock that keeps running even when the computer is turned off. There may be other icons here also, but they need not concern us now.

The centre of the taskbar is largely blank. However, when a game or program is opened on the desktop, it will also appear as a small button on the taskbar.

## WINDOWS

When the **calculator** or **Solitaire** opened, each opened in its own **window** – a small panel – on the desktop. A window may be a small part of the screen or it may fill the whole screen.

You learnt how to close those windows by clicking a little red button in the top right-hand corner.

The Desktop and Windows

4

Open **Solitaire** on your computer – if it is not already open – to learn about the main parts of a window.

### The Title Bar

The blue bar along the top of the window is the **Title bar**.

Title Bar

The title of the window appears on the left-hand end of the Title bar. In this case, you see the name of the card game, **Solitaire**. There is also a small icon representing a pack of cards.

The bar can be used to drag the window to a different part of the desktop.

### Window Buttons

There are three **Buttons** at the right-hand end of the Title bar.

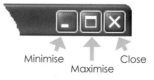

Minimise    Close
Maximise

The red button on the right is the **Close** button (do not click it for now).

The centre button is the **Maximise** button.

It enlarges – or **maximises** – the window to fill the whole desktop. Click it to see what happens.

The Desktop and Windows

4

When a window is maximised, clicking the same button again **Restores** the window to its original size. Try it now! Practise maximising and restoring to see how it works.

The left-hand button is the **Minimise** button.

The minimise button hides the window temporarily when you want to do something else on the desktop. It does not close the game (or other item). Instead, it reduces – or **minimises** – the window to become a **button** on the Taskbar. Click it now to see what happens.

Now look at the Taskbar and you will see a **Solitaire** button (with its pack of cards icon).

Click the Solitaire button and the window pops up again immediately.

Note that the button is still on the Taskbar but now it has a 'pressed in' appearance.

This is to show that the window associated with this button is open on the desktop.

> **Did you notice?** When you point to one of the buttons on the Title bar, a label pops up after a second or two to tell you what it is or what it does. Labels like this pop up when you point to other things too.

## The Menu Bar

The **Menu bar** is the pale bar immediately under the **Title bar**.

Menu Bar ⟶ | **Solitaire**  _ □ ×
Game  Help

Here you will find menus associated with each particular window.

Solitaire has only two menus, **Game** and **Help**.

The Desktop and Windows

4

Click on these words in turn, now known as the **Game Menu** and the **Help Menu**, to display the contents of each menu.

Click anywhere outside a menu, but inside the Solitaire window, to close an open menu.

## Using a Menu

You have already used the **Help** menu in Chapter 3.

Now click the **Game** menu (click on the word **Game**).

The menu appears.

The first item on the menu is **Deal**.

Click **Deal** to deal a new game of Solitaire.

(You used the **F2** key to do this in the last chapter.) The menu closes and the new game appears.

Would you like to have a different pattern for the back of the cards?

Open the **Game** menu again (click on the word **Game**).

Click **Deck....**

A new small window appears with the title **Select Card Back**. It displays a selection of patterns for the back of the cards.

Click the pattern you require.

Notice that a border appears around it to show that you have selected it.

Click the **OK** button at the bottom of the window.

The small window disappears and cards in the game now have the new pattern on the back.

**Did you notice?** There was a **Cancel** button beside the **OK** button at the bottom of the **Select Card Back** window.

Click the **Cancel** button wherever it appears in a window if you change your mind and decide not to proceed with a particular task.

## More Menu Options

You can select different options for **Solitaire** as follows.

Open the **Game** menu again.

Click **Options....**
The Options window appears.

(Remember, you can drag the Options window to a different part of the desktop if necessary.)

Click one or more options, as you require.

A dot or tick appears beside each selected item to show that it has been selected.

**Did you notice?** The items already ticked when the window opened? Those were the options in use when you were playing Solitaire earlier.

Click the **OK** button at the bottom of the window to confirm and apply your choices.

If you do not want to make any changes, click the **Cancel** button.

## Those Dots...

Why have **Deck** and **Options** in the menu got three dots after them while **Deal** has none?

It is because some menu items offer you a choice and others do not.

When you click **Deal**, for example, that instruction is carried out immediately.

A new game is dealt.

However, a menu item with three dots means that a choice has to be made, as when you selected new card patterns or other options.

When you have made your choice, you usually have to click an **OK** or **Apply** button to confirm it.

## THE HELP BUTTON

Did you understand what all the options were? If not, open the **Options** menu again, if you had closed it. Notice the button with the **question mark** on the right of the **Title bar**. It is a **Help** button.

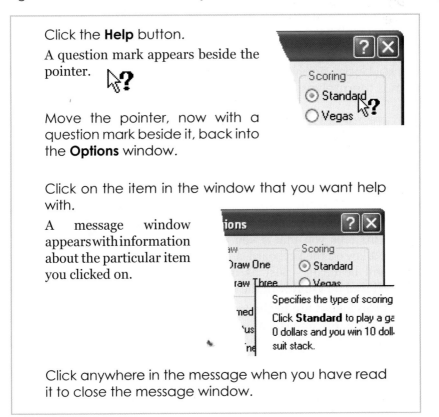

Click the **Help** button.
A question mark appears beside the pointer.

Move the pointer, now with a question mark beside it, back into the **Options** window.

Click on the item in the window that you want help with.

A message window appears with information about the particular item you clicked on.

Specifies the type of scoring

Click **Standard** to play a ga 0 dollars and you win 10 doll. suit stack.

Click anywhere in the message when you have read it to close the message window.

4

Click the **Help** button again and repeat the process for help on other items.

Click **OK** or **Cancel** to continue.

## KEYBOARD SHORTCUTS

Many menu items can be selected by pressing a key or two on the keyboard.

You do not have to use the mouse all the time and you can save yourself time and effort by using the keyboard. But how do you know which keys to press?

The keyboard equivalents of many menu items are shown in the menus themselves. Do the following.

Open the **Game** menu in Solitaire.

Look at **Deal** in the menu and notice **F2** to the right.

This tells you that if you press the **F2** key on the keyboard, a new game will be dealt – just as if you had clicked on **Deal** with the mouse.

(The F keys are in the top row on the keyboard, labelled **F1**, **F2**, **F3,** and so on).

Now click anywhere in the Solitaire window to close the menu.

Press the **F2** key on the keyboard.

A new game is dealt instantly. And you didn't have to touch the mouse or go searching through menus!

Look out for keyboard shortcuts on other menus.

## THE STATUS BAR

There is one more bar to notice in some windows. It is the **Status bar** and it is at the **bottom** of the window.

Status Bar

The **Status bar** is used to display information that may vary from time to time.

In Solitaire, the score and the time are displayed at the right-hand end of the bar.

Whether or not the Status bar in Solitaire is displayed depends on whether or not there is a tick in the little box beside **Status bar** in the **Options** window described on page 57.

The Desktop and Windows

4

## EXIT

When you closed **Solitaire** before, you clicked the **Close** button (the one with the **X** in it) at the right-hand end of the Title bar.

Games, programs and open windows can also be closed by clicking **Exit** in one of the menus.

In Solitaire, you will find **Exit** at the bottom of the **Game** menu. Clicking Exit here closes Solitaire, just as if you had clicked the **Close** button in the Title bar.

## CHANGING THE SIZE OF A WINDOW

Windows do not have to always remain the same size as when they were first opened.

You have already seen that you can maximise a window to fill the whole desktop.

Sometimes, however, you might like a window to be just a little larger so that you can see more of its contents. Or perhaps a large window with only a few items in it takes up too much space on the desktop and could be much smaller.

To change the size of a window, do the following.

Move the pointer **slowly** over the corner or side of the window.

As the pointer moves over the corner or side, it becomes a **double-headed arrow**.

Three double-headed arrows are shown on the next page, on the side, corner and bottom of a window, to show what they look like in different positions. Note that only **one** will actually appear on your screen depending on where you place and move the mouse.

The Desktop and Windows

4

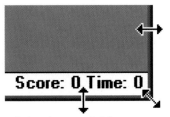

If you move the pointer too quickly, you may lose the double-headed arrow.

If that happens, move the pointer back slowly until it appears again.

When the double-headed arrow appears, **stop**, hold down the button and **drag**.

Release the mouse button when the window is the size you require.

You will notice that when you drag a side or the bottom of the window, the window is stretched to make it wider or deeper, but not both at the same time.

If you drag a corner of the window diagonally (towards or away from the opposite corner, in the direction of the arrows), both the width and depth of the window are changed together in proportion. This is often the most useful way to resize a window.

---

**Practice**

Open **Solitaire**, if it is not already open, and practise resizing the Solitaire window.

Make the window **wider**.

Make the window **deeper**.

---

The Desktop and Windows

63

4

**Maximise** and **Restore** the window to see that it returns to the size you last set.

**Undo** the changes you made by dragging the sides or bottom back to approximately where they were before.

**Resize** the window by dragging a corner.

Notice that if you make the window too small, as in the illustration below, you will not be able to see all the cards.

Finally, return the window to approximately **its original size** and **centre it** on the desktop.

Note: The **Calculator** window (and some other windows) cannot be resized or maximised.

## More than one Window

In earlier chapters, you removed the **Calculator** from the desktop by clicking its **Close** button or by clicking **Exit** in a menu. You did the same with **Solitaire**.

But it is not necessary to close one window before you open the other. Both can be open at the same time or you can minimise one while you work with the other.

4

Try the following.

Open both **Calculator** and **Solitaire** (if they are not already open).

One will probably be in front of the other, making it difficult to see or work with the one underneath.

Click anywhere on the window that is underneath.

Notice that the window you clicked on now comes to the front and that the window that was previously in front is now underneath.

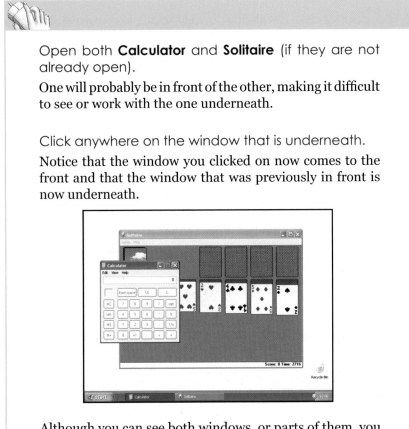

Although you can see both windows, or parts of them, you can only work with one at a time – the one that is in front. Thus the window in front is known as the active window.

Notice that the **Title bar**, **menus** and other parts of the window underneath are faint, to show that it is **inactive**.

Clicking anywhere on an inactive window brings it to the front and makes it active again.

4

## TASKBAR BUTTONS

If you cannot see a window underneath because it is totally covered by another window, minimise the active window. (Click the **Minimise** button).

The window underneath is then revealed and you can drag it to another part of the desktop.

The minimised window appears as a button on the Taskbar, as explained earlier, see page 54.

Active   Inactive

Click a **button** on the Taskbar to activate a window (bring it to the front) or to switch between active windows.

Restore the window that you minimised by clicking its **button** on the Taskbar.

Practise minimising and restoring the two windows. Notice that you can minimise both of them to clear the desktop.

Practise moving the windows to different parts of the desktop so that they overlap or do not overlap (if possible).

Practise bringing an overlapped window to the front so that it can all be seen and then practise bringing the original window back to the front again.

In this chapter, you have learnt...

- about the desktop and what it is.

- that the desktop should be kept tidy and uncluttered.

- about the taskbar and what it contains.

- about windows and their parts.

Do you remember...

- how to use a menu?

- how to use the **Help** button?

- how to change the size of a window?

- how to work with more than one window at a time?

The Desktop and Windows

4

# CHAPTER 5
# Painting and Drawing

This chapter shows you how to use a program on the computer to draw a picture.
You will use the mouse to select tools and colours and to draw simple shapes.

# Painting and Drawing

Now that you are comfortable using the mouse, have learnt how to use windows and menus, and know how the desktop is arranged, you can use your new-found skills to do something creative with the computer – paint a picture!

A program called **Paint** will help you to develop your skills further. It is called a **program** to distinguish it from a **game**, such as Solitaire.

You will use the **Paint** program to paint a simple picture. You will select brushes, colours, and so on using the mouse. Then, again using the mouse, you will paint your picture.

## OPENING PAINT

**Paint** is stored in the **Accessories** folder. You find and open Paint in the same way that you found and opened the calculator.

Proceed as follows.

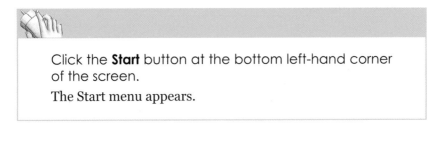

Click the **Start** button at the bottom left-hand corner of the screen.

The Start menu appears.

71

5

Point to **All Programs**.

All Programs is highlighted and the Programs menu appears.

Point to **Accessories** in the All Programs menu.

Accessories is highlighted and the Accessories menu appears.

Point to **Paint** in the Accessories menu.

Paint is highlighted.

Click **Paint** to open it.

Paint appears in its own window, just as the **calculator** and the **Solitaire** game did when they were opened.

## THE PAINT WINDOW

The main (white) part of the window represents the **blank paper,** or **canvas,** on which you will draw/paint. The size of the canvas can be changed by dragging the bottom right-hand corner of the canvas, only if you want to.

The size of the window can be adjusted, if necessary, as described in Chapter 4, on page 62.

The tools (brushes, pencils, etc.) are arranged down the left side of the window.

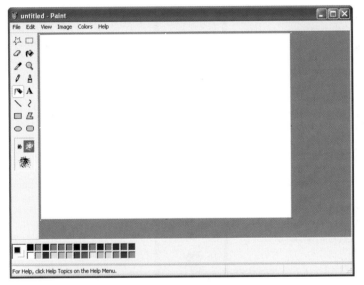

A selection of colours that you can choose from appears along the bottom.

You will use the mouse as if it were a pencil or a brush to draw the picture by **pointing**, **clicking** and **dragging**. As you move the mouse on the mouse mat, the pencil or brush that you have selected will do the drawing on the screen.

Painting and Drawing

5

## THE TOOLS

The tools buttons are described here. Each button has an icon on it to remind you of the tool it represents.

| | |
|---|---|
| Select an irregular area | Select a rectangular area |
| Eraser for rubbing out | Paint Bucket for filling with colour |
| Eye Dropper for picking up colours | Magnifying Glass for a closer look |
| Pencil for drawing | Brush for painting |
| Spray can (Airbrush) | Write on your drawing |
| Draw a straight line | Draw a curved line |
| Draw a rectangle | Draw an irregular shape |
| Draw an ellipse or circle | Draw a box with round corners |
| Choose a tool size (some tools only) | |

## Select a Tool

Click any tool.

Notice that it now has a 'pressed in' appearance like the **Spray Can** tool in the illustration on page 74. This shows that you have selected it for use.

Notice also that, when you select the Spray Can, there are three different spray sizes available, as shown in the little panel under the tools.

Click a size to select it. It will then be highlighted to show that it has been selected, like the middle size in the illustration on page 74.

Click on different tools. You will notice that only one tool can be selected at any one time.

## Select a Colour

A selection of colours is shown at the bottom of the window.

Click a colour to select it.

Notice that the colour you select is shown on the very left of the colours panel (arrowed in the illustration).

For Help, click Help Topics on the Help Menu.

Notice also that a reminder of where you can find help appears at the bottom of the window.

Painting and Drawing

5

## Start Drawing

Why not start with spray painting?

Click the **Spray Can** tool to select it. (Paint says it's an **Airbrush**, but it looks like a spray can.)

Click the middle size of spray in the size panel under the tools.

Click the colour **Red** at the bottom of the window to select it.

Move the mouse over into the blank canvas area.

Notice that the pointer is now in the shape of a spray can. Try to write your name in capitals. For each part of a letter, do the following.

Hold down the mouse button.

Move the mouse.

Release the button.

The slower you move the mouse, the more paint is sprayed, just like a real spray can!

Click the **Eraser** tool and use it, like the spray can, to erase any untidy bits of what you have drawn.

Select different colours for different letters.

Draw a line underneath your name.

## Begin Again?

Would you like to erase everything and start all over again?

Go to the **Image** menu and click on **Clear Image**.

## SELECTING AND MOVING

You can move part of your drawing if you wish.

First click the **rectangular selection button** at the top of the tools panel (the right-hand one – see illustration).

Click and hold down the mouse button on the page where you want to begin.

Painting and Drawing

5

Then drag diagonally. You will see a dotted rectangle appearing as you drag.

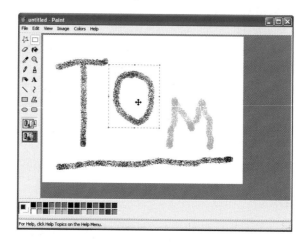

Release the mouse button when the dotted rectangle encloses the area that you want to move.

If the rectangle is not exactly where you had intended, click once anywhere else in the Paint window and start again.

Move the pointer into the dotted rectangle.
It changes shape to arrows pointing in all directions.

Hold down the mouse button and drag to move your selection.

Release the button to place the selection in its new position.

## More Practice

Begin again and try writing your name with joined letters, as if you were holding a pen.

Use brushes of different kinds.

First click a brush button to select it. Then click in the selection panel under the tools to select the type of brush you want to use. Use different brushes to produce different effects. Use the pencil for fine work.

When you are finished practising letters, draw a simple picture.

# USING SHAPES

Draw simple shapes and colour them in, as in the following example.

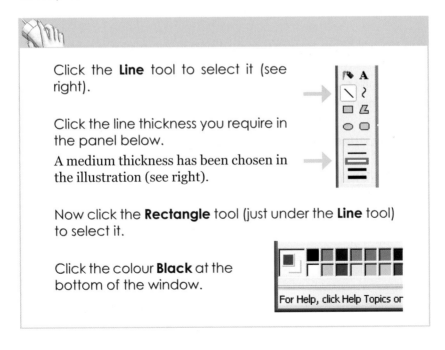

Click the **Line** tool to select it (see right).

Click the line thickness you require in the panel below.

A medium thickness has been chosen in the illustration (see right).

Now click the **Rectangle** tool (just under the **Line** tool) to select it.

Click the colour **Black** at the bottom of the window.

For Help, click Help Topics or

Painting and Drawing

5

Move the cursor over the blank canvas.
Notice that it is now in the shape of a **crosshair**. +

Hold down the mouse button and drag diagonally to draw a large rectangle.

Release the button when the rectangle is the size you require.
The rectangle is drawn with the line thickness you have selected.

Select a thinner or thicker line, if you prefer, before you click the rectangle tool to draw the shape.

## UNDOING AN ACTION

You do not have to erase everything if you make a mistake.

Go to the **Edit** menu and click **Undo** to undo your last action.

Click **Undo** again to undo the action before that.

Click **Repeat** in the Edit menu to cancel (or 'redo') an **Undo** action.

5

## FILL A SHAPE WITH COLOUR

Use **Paint Bucket** to fill an enclosed shape with colour.

Click **Paint Bucket** to select it.

Click the colour you require.

Move the pointer, now a paint bucket, into the shape.

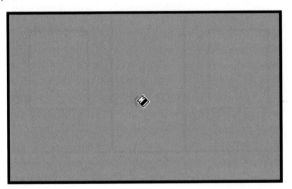

Click the mouse button to fill the shape with colour.

Note that if the shape is not fully enclosed – if you have erased part of the edge to make a hole, for example – the colour will 'leak' out through the hole. If that happens, use **Undo** as described on page 80. Then fix the hole and try again.

Would you prefer a different colour?

Click on a different colour to select it and then click inside the shape again.

Painting and Drawing

5

### Draw a House

Imagine that the coloured rectangle you have just drawn is the front wall of a house.

Now draw three smaller rectangles to represent two windows and a door.

Look back at the previous sections if you have forgotten how to do the following.

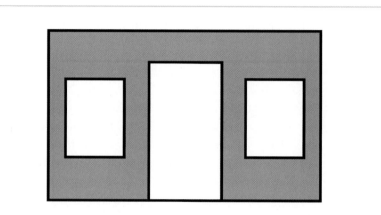

Select the **Line** tool.

Select a line thickness and colour.

Select the **Rectangle** tool.

Draw a rectangle.
And don't forget: use **Undo** to correct mistakes!

## Add Detail

Use the **Line** tool to put cross pieces on the windows.

Use the **Rectangle** tool to draw a letterbox on the door.

Use the **Circle/Ellipse** tool to draw a door knob.

Use the **Paint Bucket** to paint the door a colour of your choice.

## Drawing the Roof

Drawing the roof is a little more complicated because it is an irregular shape. To avoid disturbing the parts of the house you have already drawn, you will draw the roof above the existing work and lower it into position later (see page 86).

Proceed as follows and remember to use the **Undo** button if things do not go right the first time.

Click the **Irregular Shape** (Polygon) tool (just to the right of the rectangle tool) to select it.

Check that black is selected as the colour.

Now look at the illustration on the next page and follow the steps to draw the roof. The lines will appear one by one as you proceed.

Painting and Drawing

5

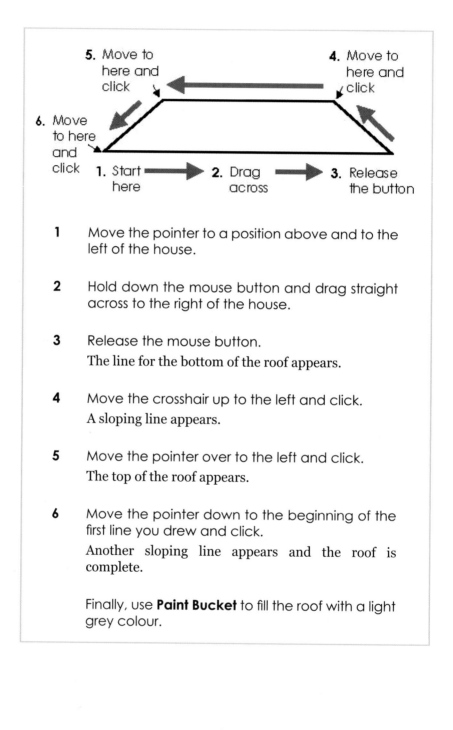

1    Move the pointer to a position above and to the left of the house.

2    Hold down the mouse button and drag straight across to the right of the house.

3    Release the mouse button.
The line for the bottom of the roof appears.

4    Move the crosshair up to the left and click.
A sloping line appears.

5    Move the pointer over to the left and click.
The top of the roof appears.

6    Move the pointer down to the beginning of the first line you drew and click.
Another sloping line appears and the roof is complete.

Finally, use **Paint Bucket** to fill the roof with a light grey colour.

Remember that there must not be a 'hole' in the outline of the roof or the colour will 'leak' out through it onto the whole page.

## Selecting the Roof

In order to move the roof down onto the house, you must first select it using the rectangular selection tool.

Click the rectangular selection tool at the top of the tools panel to select it.

Two coloured buttons under the tools panel determine whether the roof and the white 'paper' surrounding it are moved or just the roof alone.

Click the lower coloured button below the tools to move the roof alone, without its surrounding white space.

Move back over the canvas.
Notice that the pointer becomes a **crosshair**.

Start below and to one side of one of the 'pointed' corners of the roof.

Press and **hold down** the button on the mouse.

Still holding down the mouse button, drag diagonally upwards.

Keep dragging until the roof is enclosed by a dotted line, as in the illustration.

Release the mouse button.

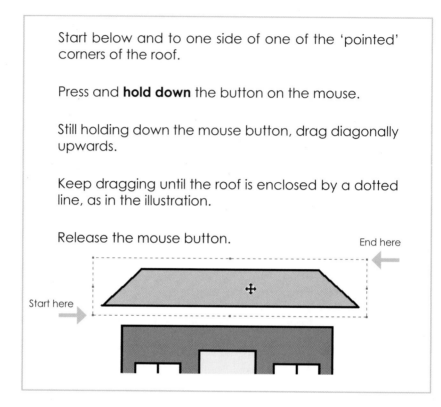

## Moving the Roof

Now you can move the roof into position.

Move the pointer until it is inside the dotted area. It becomes a cross with arrows pointing in all directions, as in the illustration above.

Hold down the mouse button and drag the roof down into position.

Release the mouse button when the roof is where you want it to be.

Click anywhere outside the dotted area to finish.

If you did not place the roof exactly where you intended, use **Undo** and try again.

## The Final Touches

Will your house be warm?

Draw a small rectangle for a chimney and fill it with a medium shade of grey.

Use the **Spray Can** to add a wisp of light grey smoke!

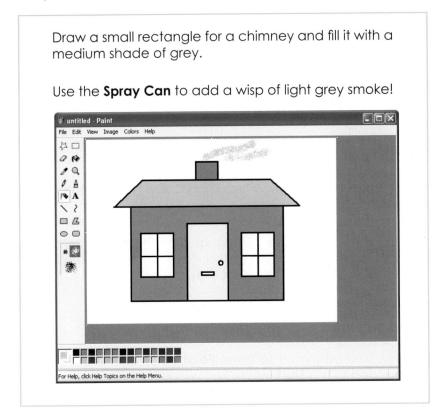

Painting and Drawing

5

### Saving Your House

After all this effort, you might like to save your picture so that you can come back to it again. Do the following.

Click **Save** in the **File** menu to open the **Save As** window.

Go to the keyboard and type the word *House* (you do not have to click on anything first). If you do not type anything, the picture will automatically be called **Untitled**.

Click the **Save** button in the bottom right-hand corner of the Save window (or the **Cancel** button if you change your mind).

Your picture is saved on the computer in a folder called **My Pictures** with the name 'House' (or '**Untitled**' if you did not type anything).

### Closing Paint

Close **Paint** in the same way that you closed the **calculator** and **Solitaire**.

Click the red **Close** button at the top right-hand corner of the Paint window (the one with the **X** in it).

### Reopening Paint

The next time you want to open **Paint**, you will find that it has been added to the **Start** menu. You will not need to go through the various menus to find it.

Painting and Drawing

5

Do the following.

Click the **Start** button to display the Start menu.

Point to **Paint** to highlight it.

Click to open Paint.

## Finding Your Picture Again

You may want to look at your **House** picture again or to continue working on it.

This is what to do.

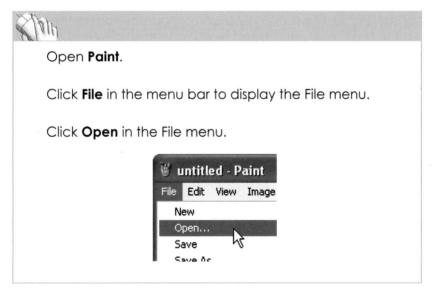

Open **Paint**.

Click **File** in the menu bar to display the File menu.

Click **Open** in the File menu.

Painting and Drawing

5

The Open window appears.

Paint automatically looks in the **My Pictures** folder and displays the pictures it finds there.

Click **House** to select it.

Click the **Open** button at the bottom right-hand corner of the window.

The House picture appears in the Paint window and you can continue to work on it as before.

*Alternatively,* click on the name of your picture if it is listed at the bottom of the **File** menu. (The computer remembers the most recent items you have been working with and keeps a list of them there.)

Saving and reopening as described above is based on the assumption that **My Pictures** is where pictures are normally stored on the computer. If this setting has been changed on your computer, your picture may be stored somewhere else in a different folder.

Painting and Drawing

5

## Saving Again

After you have carried out your house improvements, you will want to save them.

Click **Save** in the **File** menu, as before.

This time, however, nothing seems to happen. The **Save As** window does not appear.

The computer already knows the name of the file and where it is to be saved and it does not have to ask you for these details again.

Don't worry, your improvements really have been saved.

Painting and Drawing

5

In this chapter, you have learnt...

- how to open a program.

- about using different tools.

- how to use shapes and colours.

Do you remember...

- how to select a tool to use?

- how to use the undo button?

- how to clear everything and start again?

- how to save your picture?

- how to find an reopen your picture again?

Painting and Drawing

5

# CHAPTER 6

# Playing a Game

This chapter introduces you to a very popular use of computers – playing games!

# Playing a Game

Pinball is a game that is found in amusement arcades and other places. It uses a small sloping table covered with pins or other obstructions. Like Solitaire, Pinball can also be played on the computer using a picture of a real pinball table.

## THE GAME

To play the game, a ball is launched around the table. It bounces off the objects as it gradually rolls down towards a hole at the bottom. Every object hit by the ball scores a number of points. The object is to get the highest score possible by bouncing the ball back up the table, using two flippers, before it can fall into a hole at the bottom. Just as with a real pinball table, the computer provides lots of flashing lights and sounds as you play.

Playing a Game

6

## Opening Pinball

To open **Pinball** for the first time, proceed as follows.

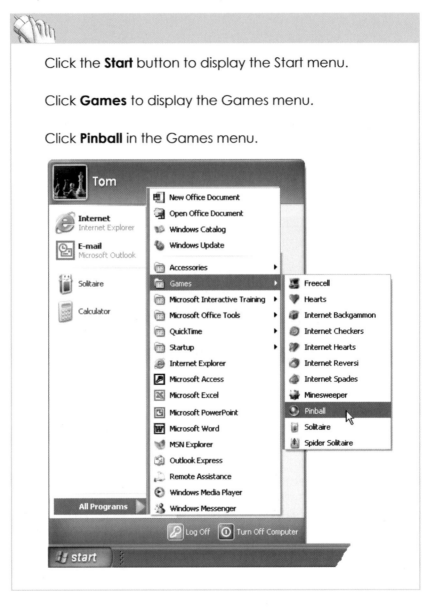

Click the **Start** button to display the Start menu.

Click **Games** to display the Games menu.

Click **Pinball** in the Games menu.

The 3D Pinball picture appears for a moment or two before the 3D Pinball window proper appears.

## The Pinball Window

The Pinball table appears in the left of the window. Notice the (small) ball near the bottom right of the table and the flippers at the bottom centre.

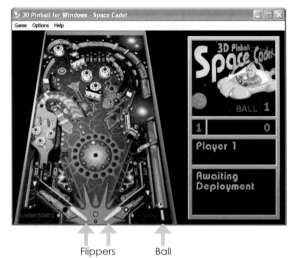

Flippers          Ball

The right of the window displays information about the number of balls used (you start with Ball 1), the score (0 to start with) and other information.

## The Flippers

The flippers are operated by pressing the **Z** and **?** keys on the keyboard. (The **?** key is the one with the question mark on it.) They are both on the row above the **Space Bar** (the long key at the bottom of the keyboard), on the left and right.

Playing a Game

6

Press them now to see how the flippers move.

## Starting Pinball

Press and release the **Space Bar** to launch the ball.

Spring

As you hold down the space bar, see how the 'spring' under the ball is compressed.

The longer you hold down the space bar, the more the spring is compressed and the faster the ball is launched when you release the space bar.

## Playing Pinball

Watch the ball as it bounces around on the table. Notice how the score – shown in the right of the window – increases as the ball encounters various objects.

If the ball rolls down over one of the flippers, press the **Z** or **?** key on the keyboard to flip the ball back up again.

Z key   ? key

## Lost Ball?

Did you lose your ball?

Press the **Space bar** to launch another one.

### New Game

Press the **F2** key on the keyboard to start a new game.
(Do you remember doing this in Solitaire?)

## SOUNDS AND MUSIC

The **Options** menu enables you to turn **sounds** and **music** on or off. If there is a tick beside an item, it is turned on.

If there is no tick beside an item, click on it to turn it on.

Click again to remove the tick and turn it off.

## FULL SCREEN

Click **Full Screen** in the **Options** menu to enlarge Pinball to fill the screen.

Alternatively, press the **F4** key at the top of the keyboard.

**Did you notice** the **F4** keyboard shortcut in the menu?

**Did you notice** that the menus are hidden when Pinball fills the screen. How can you see them again?

Playing a Game

6

99

Press the **Alt** key (to the left of the space bar) to display the menus again.

Alternatively, press the **F4** key to reduce the window to its original size.

You will find it more convenient to use the **F4** key to switch between sizes.

## HIGH SCORES

The High Scores window may appear if you achieve a high score.

Type your name using the keyboard and then click the **OK** button.

Click the **Cancel** button if you do not want to record your score.

Click the **Clear** button only if you want to clear all the high score records.

You can select **High Scores** in the **Game** menu to check the high scores at any time.

Playing a Game

6

100

## GETTING HELP

Click **Help Topics** in the **Help** menu for help and information about Pinball.

Alternatively, press the **F1** key on the keyboard.

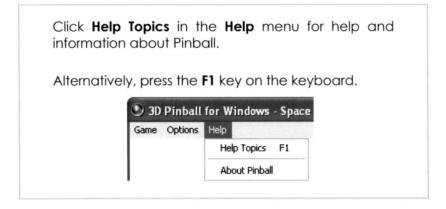

Using Help for Pinball is similar to using Help for **Solitaire** and other programs. Look back at Chapter 3, page 43, if you need to refresh your memory about how to use Help.

## CLOSING PINBALL

To close **Pinball** when you are finished, click the red **Close** button in the top right-hand corner.

It is the button with the **X** in it.

Playing a Game

6

101

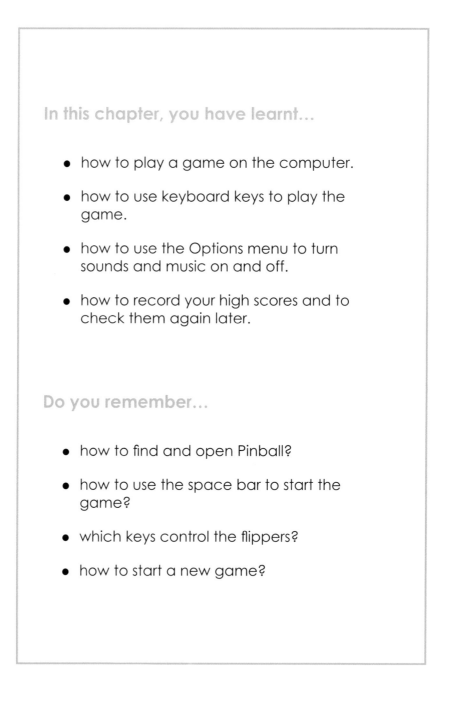

In this chapter, you have learnt...

- how to play a game on the computer.

- how to use keyboard keys to play the game.

- how to use the Options menu to turn sounds and music on and off.

- how to record your high scores and to check them again later.

Do you remember...

- how to find and open Pinball?

- how to use the space bar to start the game?

- which keys control the flippers?

- how to start a new game?

Playing a Game

6

## CHAPTER 7

# The Keyboard

This chapter briefly describes the keyboard and tells you about some of the keys that you will use most often.

# The Keyboard

If you have used a typewriter, you will see that the computer keyboard is essentially the same, but with a number of extra keys. There is also a number pad – like a calculator – on the right (but not on a laptop computer, where there is not enough space for it).

The keyboard is often referred to as the **QWERTY** keyboard because of the order of the first six letters in the top row of letters.

Learning to use the keyboard is just learning to type. There are several computer typing courses, programs that you buy and install on your computer to teach yourself to type.

The keyboard is displayed on the screen, with instructions and exercises.

It works as though you had your own personal tutor.

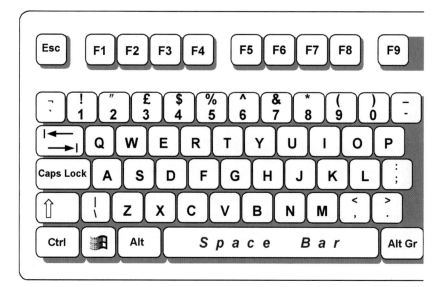

## THE KEYS ON THE KEYBOARD

The keyboard is shown here split over two pages for clarity.

Your own keyboard may be slightly different to the one shown here, perhaps with one or two keys in different places.

The principal typing keys – on the main part of the keyboard – are arranged in the same way as they are on a typewriter.

Not all the keys will have printed labels as in the illustrations. The **Space bar**, for example is usually left blank.

Most of the keys can be used for more than one purpose but only some of them are labelled. The second row of keys from the top has two symbols on each key, for example.

Pressing a key produces the lower symbol but holding down the **Shift** key while you press a key produces the upper one.

Shift key

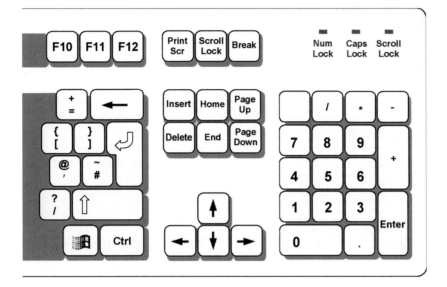

Pressing any letter key produces a 'small' (lower case) letter but when you hold down the shift key, a 'capital' (upper case) letter is produced.

Notice that there is a **Shift** key at each side of the keyboard.

Shift key

Press the **Caps Lock** key once and all the text that you type next will be in capital letters.

Press the **Caps Lock** key again to resume typing normally.

Other keys that you may need to use are the **Alt** key and the **Tab** key.

Tab key

The Keyboard

107

## Special Keys

You will only need to use many of the extra keys on the computer keyboard occasionally, if at all. It is not necessary to know what they are all for just now.

The keys numbered from **F1** to **F12** at the top of the keyboard are only used by some programs. In **Solitaire**, for example, you used **F2** to deal a new game.

The number keys on the keypad on the right are convenient for typing numbers if you are used to using a calculator. You can use the number keys on the main keyboard just as well.

Small lights at the top right of the keyboard show that certain keys are being used. If you press the **Caps Lock** key, for example, the **Caps Lock** light comes on to remind you.

Two important keys that you will use constantly are **Return** and **Backspace**. They are usually larger that the other keys for this reason. The **Delete** key is also one that you will use often.

Backspace key          Delete key

Return key

The group of four **Arrow** keys are used to move around in a piece of text. They are also useful for moving objects such as lines or pictures.

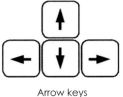

Arrow keys

In this chapter, you have learnt...

- about the keyboard and its keys.

- about some of the keys that you will use often.

- about the special keys.

Do you remember...

- where the **Return** key is?

- where the **Backspace** key is?

- where the **Arrow** keys are?

The Keyboard

7

# CHAPTER 8
# Writing a Letter

This chapter shows you how to use a word processor on your computer to write a short letter.

# Writing a Letter

A computer program called a **word processor** is used to write letters and to prepare documents of all kinds. In this chapter, you will use the **Microsoft Works** word processor.

Using a computer has many advantages, even if your typing skills are limited.

Typing errors are very easy to correct.

The computer can correct spelling mistakes for you.

You can easily keep copies of all your letters.

Copies of letters can be sent to different people. Some details can be changed to suit each person, without having to type out everything again.

## OPENING MICROSOFT WORKS

This is how to find **Microsoft Works** if you are opening it for the first time.

Click the **Start** button.

The Start menu appears.

Point to **All Programs**.

All Programs is highlighted and the Programs menu appears.

Point to **Microsoft Works** in the All Programs menu.

The Microsoft Works menu appears.

Click **Microsoft Works Word Processor** to open it.

It appears in its own window, just as the calculator and Solitaire did.

Writing a Letter

Click the **Maximise** button if the window does not fill the screen.

The full screen size is more convenient to use for most documents.

## The Microsoft Works Window

If there is a large panel – **Works Help** – on the right, as in the illustration below, click the panel's **Close** button (arrowed) to make more space available on the screen. You do not need these items for the moment.

You can display the panel again later, if necessary, by clicking the round red button with the question mark on the toolbar.

Close button

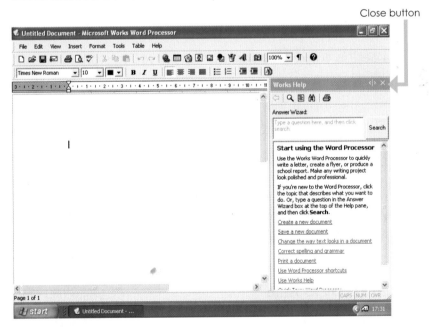

At the top of the window is the blue **Title Bar**, as in the other windows you have seen. Here the title is **Untitled Document**.

Writing a Letter

8

The **Menu Bar** is directly underneath the title bar. There are several menus along the bar.

Underneath the Menu Bar are two **Toolbars**. These have buttons on them, which enable you to perform varoius actions.

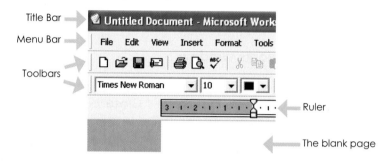

The large white space which fills most of the window is the **Blank Page**, the (so far) **Untitled Document**. This is where you will write your letter.

Notice the flashing **cursor**, waiting for you to start typing.

Move up

Across the top of the blank page is a numbered **Ruler** to indicate margins and other information.

At the right-hand side of the window is a vertical **Scroll Bar** with small scroll arrows at the top and bottom.

You will click the **Scroll Arrows** to move the page up and down in the window as necessary.

Move down

## Getting Ready to Write

The top of the blank page is up against the ruler, as in the illustration on the next page.

(Don't worry if you can't see the edges of the page on your own screen.)

8

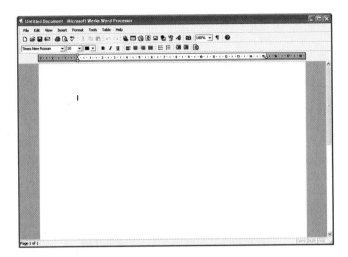

You can move down (and back up) the page by using the scroll arrows.

Point to the **Move Down** arrow on the scroll bar and **hold down** the mouse button.

The page moves up until you come to the bottom of the page.

Release the mouse button.

Go back to the top of the page

Point to the **Move Up** arrow on the scroll bar and **hold down** the mouse button.

The page moves down until you come to the top of the page.

Release the mouse button.

Writing a letter

8

## Larger Icons

The icons on the toolbars at the top of the window can be enlarged so that you can see them more easily.

Open the **View** menu (click the word **View** on the menu bar).

Point to **Toolbars** in the menu to display the toolbars menu.

Click **Large Icons** in the toolbar menu.

Untitled Document - Microsoft Works Word Proces

File | Edit | View | Insert | Format | Tools | Table | Help

Toolbars ▶ | ✓ Standard
✓ Ruler | ✓ Formatting
Times New R; | ✓ Status Bar | Large Icons

¶ All Characters
Header and Footer

Zoom...

Click **Large Icons** again if you want to return the icons to their original size.

## Typing Hints

You do not need to do anything in particular before you type. Just go to the keyboard and start typing.

As you type, the text appears on the blank page on the screen.

To make a capital letter, hold down the **Shift** key while you type the letter.

Shift key

When you come to the end of a line, your text automatically goes on to the next line as you type.

Writing a Letter

8

To start a new paragraph, press the **Return** key.

To add some space before you type the next paragraph, press the **Return** key again to insert a blank line.

Return key

To remove a letter or a blank line that you have added by mistake, press the **Backspace** key.

Backspace key

## Start Writing

You will type a brief letter to Catherine, thanking her for an invitation.

Do not be worried about making mistakes. You will be able to correct them later.

Go to the keyboard and proceed as follows on the next page.

Writing a Letter

8

119

Type **Hillview House.**

Press the **Return** key to go on to the next line.

Press the **Return** key again to insert a blank line.

Type **5th October** (or the current date if you wish).

Press the **Return** key three times to add blank lines and move down the page.

Type **Dear Catherine.**

Press the **Return** key and continue as before, adding blank lines as you require, completing the letter as follows.

**Thank you for the invitation to the Golf Club.**

**Regards**

**Tom**

## Undoing Mistakes

It is very easy to undo a mistake by using the **Undo** button under the menu bar at the top of the window. It looks like a small arrow curving around to the left. Clicking the button cancels the last action you made.

Click the **Undo** button to undo your last action.

Click the **Undo** button again to undo what you did before that.

Undo   Redo

The **Redo** button, a small arrow curving around to the right, cancels what the **Undo** button did, if you changed your mind about undoing an action.

Try clicking the **Undo** button once or twice to see it working.

Then click the **Redo** button to see the Undos cancelled and the original restored.

## New Pointers

**Did you notice** that now different pointers appear on the screen as you move the mouse?

When you move the mouse off the page, it is the usual **arrow** shape.

When you move back over the page, it is the shape of a capital '**I**'.

There is also a flashing vertical line after the last thing that you typed.

It marks the place where whatever you type next will appear. It is called the **Insertion Point**.

## Correcting Errors

Suppose that you typed a **h** in Hillview – like this, Hillvi**h**ew – and want to correct it.

Writing a letter

8

The **Undo** button may remove the entire line, when all you want to do is remove a single letter.

Proceed as follows.

Move the mouse so that the **Pointer** is between the **h** and the **e** and click the mouse button.

Pointer

Hillvih|ew

Now move the mouse away.

Flashing insertion pointer

If you do not move it away, the **Insertion Point** and the **pointer** will be on top of each other, which would be confusing.

Notice that the **insertion point** is now flashing between the two letters and that the pointer is where you moved it to (as in the illustration).

Press the **Backspace** key to delete the letter **h**.

Backspace key

Note that the **Backspace** key deletes the letter to the left of the Insertion Point. If you want to delete a letter to the right of the Insertion Point, press the **Delete** key.

Delete key

## The Arrow Keys

Another way to move the insertion point is to use the **Arrow** keys at the bottom of the keyboard. They have arrows pointing up, down, left and right.

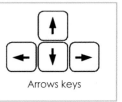

Press the **Up** key to move the Insertion Point up line by line.

Press the **Down** key to move it down line by line.

Arrows keys

Writing a Letter

8

Press the **Left** or **Right** keys to move it left or right in the line.

## Continue Typing

You must reposition the **Insertion Point** before you continue typing. Otherwise, what you type next will appear where the Insertion Point was last – in the middle of **Hillview**, for example. Just move the mouse and click with the **Pointer** wherever you want to continue.

> **Note:**  Click anywhere in the white space to the right of a line to type at the end of the line. You do not have to click right up against the last letter in the line.

## Preparing to Save Your Letter

Before going any further, your letter needs to be stored – or **saved** – on the computer. Then you can turn off the computer safely at any time. The next time you switch on the computer, you will be able to return to the letter, add to it or make any changes that may be necessary before you print it out and post it.

To save your letter, do the following.

Click the **Save** button on the toolbar at the top of the window. It resembles a floppy disk.

The **Save As** window appears.

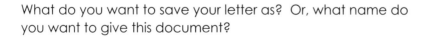

What do you want to save your letter as?  Or, what name do you want to give this document?

8

## Giving Your Letter a Name

Microsoft Works inserts '**Untitled Document'** in the **File name** box at the bottom of the window, trying to be helpful.

This is rarely appropriate. Every letter you save would have the same name – '**Untitled Document**'.

Go to the keyboard and type **Catherine**.

You do not have to touch the mouse or click anywhere first.

Whatever you type will replace 'Untitled Document' in the **File Name** box.

| Save As | | ? X |
|---|---|---|
| Save in: My Documents | ▼ ← 🗀 📄 🞅▼ | |
| 🗀 My eBooks | | |
| 🗀 My Music | | |
| 🗀 My Pictures | | |
| File name: Untitled Document | | Save |
| Save as type: Works Document (*.wps) ▼ | | Cancel |
| | | Template... |

## Where Will Your Letter be Saved?

Look at the **Save in** box at the top of the window. The word processor has already decided to save the letter in a folder called **My Documents**. We shall accept this for now and no changes have to be made.

## Saving Your Letter

Now that you have given your letter a name and know where it will be saved, you can click the **Save** button at the bottom right-hand corner of the window. Your letter is saved and the **Save As** window closes.

| Save |
| Cancel |
| Template... |

Remember, you can click the **Cancel** button if you change your mind.

## Closing and Reopening

Many people have two problems when they want to find a document that they have already saved on the computer.

They cannot remember the **name** of the document.

They do not know **where** it was saved.

This is usually because they just clicked the **Save** button without giving the document a name or checking to see where it was being saved.

It is **vitally important** to give your documents **meaningful names** that you will recognise when you are searching for them again.

It is **equally important** to know **where they are saved** so that you will know where to look for them later.

For now, you will close **Microsoft Works** and reopen it (just to practise starting from the beginning again).

In Chapter 9, you will find and reopen your letter to Catherine. You will then make some changes to the letter and save it again.

Writing a letter

8

### Closing Microsoft Works

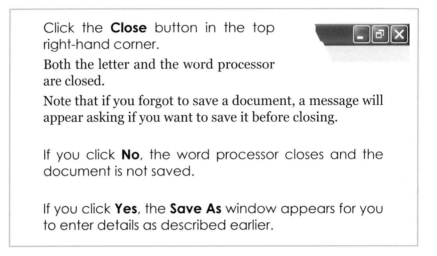

Click the **Close** button in the top right-hand corner.

Both the letter and the word processor are closed.

Note that if you forgot to save a document, a message will appear asking if you want to save it before closing.

If you click **No**, the word processor closes and the document is not saved.

If you click **Yes**, the **Save As** window appears for you to enter details as described earlier.

### Reopening the Word Processor

The next time you want to open the **Microsoft Works word processor**, you should find it on the **Start** menu.

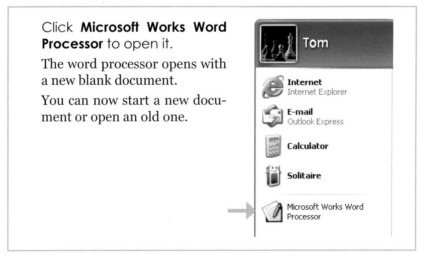

Click **Microsoft Works Word Processor** to open it.

The word processor opens with a new blank document.

You can now start a new document or open an old one.

In this chapter, you have learnt...

- about the Microsoft Works word processor.

- about commonly used items in the word processor window.

- about giving your documents meaningful names.

- about knowing where your documents are saved.

Do you remember...

- how to open, close and reopen Microsoft Works?

- how to make the toolbar icons larger?

- how to use the **Return** key to insert blank lines?

- how to undo mistakes?

- how to correct errors?

Writing a letter

8

# CHAPTER 9
# Editing a Document

This chapter shows you how to reopen a document you have saved previously and how to make changes and additions to it.

# Editing a Document

The brief letter that you wrote to Catherine has been saved and is safely stored away. Now you realise that some of the details need to be changed. You will edit (make changes to) the letter to Catherine and, in the process, learn a number of editing and word processing skills.

## CHANGES

In general, it is best to type out the text of a document first and then make changes later.

Trying to do both at the same time can slow you down.

This is what your letter will look like when you have finished.

### Hillview House
5th October

Dear Kathleen,

Thank you for your invitation to the Hillview House Golf Club.

I shall be at the main entrance at *noon* on <u>Saturday</u>.

Regards
Tom

131

9

Now, with your computer switched on again – if you had switched it off – you are ready to find and reopen your letter.

## FINDING A RECENT DOCUMENT

Microsoft Works keeps a list of the most recent documents that you were working on.

This makes it easy to find and open them again.

Open **Microsoft Works**, if it is not already open.

Open the **File** menu (click the word **File** in the menu bar – all letters and documents are files).

Look at the bottom of the **File** menu and you will see a list of recent files, giving their locations and names.

Click the **Catherine** file to open it.

The letter appears just as it was when you saved it.

# FINDING AN OLDER DOCUMENT

If the document you want to open is not on the list of recent files, do the following.

Click the **Open** button on the toolbar. It is in the shape of an opening folder.

The Open window appears. It is very similar to the **Save As** window.

Look at the **Look in** box at the top of the window. The **My Documents** folder is already in the box. Microsoft Works looks there first.

A list of the items in the My Documents folder appears in the main part of the window. You will see *Catherine* with a little Works icon beside it.

Click **Catherine** to select it (you do not have to type anything in the **File name** box at the bottom of the window).

Editing a Document

9

Click the **Open** button at the bottom right-hand corner of the window.

The Open window closes and the letter to Catherine appears, just as you had saved it.

**Tip:** Double-click **Catherine** to open the file instantly.

## MAKING CHANGES

Now that you have reopened the letter to Catherine, you can make changes to it or add some extra information.

Place the **Pointer** between the words 'the' and 'golf'.

Click the mouse button.

Move the mouse away and you will see the **Insertion Point** flashing between the words.

Go to the keyboard, type the word 'Hillview', remembering to start with a space, if necessary.

The sentence now reads: Thank you for the invitation to the Hillview golf club.

## SAVING THE CHANGES

It is good practice to save your work regularly when you are working on a document. Then, if anything should happen, the document will be up-to-date as far as the last time you saved it.

Editing a Document

9

Click the **Save** button on the toolbar.

Nothing appears to happen but your changes have actually been saved. The reason nothing appeared to happen is that Works already knows the title of the document and also where it is to be saved. You entered this information the first time you saved it. Now, it does not have to ask you for these details again.

## ADD MORE TEXT

Add another line with some more information as follows.

Click with the mouse anywhere in the blank space to the right of 'club' and then move the mouse away.

The **Insertion Point** appears at the end of 'club'. Notice that you did not have to click right up against the word 'club'. Anywhere in the white space will do as long as the pointer is level with the line of text.

If you click too high or low, the insertion point will appear on the line above or below. If that happens, just try again.

Press the **Return** key to move to the next line.

Type 'I shall be at main entrance at noon on Saturday'.

Click the **Save** button to save your work.

Editing a Document

9

## CHECK

Have your changes really been saved? It is easy to check.

> Close the letter by clicking the red **Close** button.
>
> Then reopen the letter as described earlier. You will see that you letter now includes the changes that you made.

Now you will do a little more editing to explore some of the other uses of a word processor.

## CHANGE THE FONT

The font (typeface) in Word is usually set to **Times New Roman** and the size of the letters to **12 point** (the **point** is a measurement used by printers).

This information appears on the **Toolbar** at the top-left of the window.

Change both the font in the address at the top of the letter to Catherine as follows.

Font          Size

> Open the letter to **Catherine**, if you have not opened it already.
>
> Move the pointer to the left of 'Hillview House'.
>
> Notice that the pointer, which was previously pointing to the left, is now pointing to the right.

Click the mouse button.

'Hillview House' is now selected and has a band of colour through it. If you clicked too high or low, try again.

Click the small arrow button (it is very small) at the right of the **Times New Roman** box on the toolbar. A list of fonts appears.

Click **Arial** to select the Arial font (use the scroll arrows on the right of the list to find it, if necessary).

Notice that 'Hillview House' has changed to the new font and **Arial** has replaced **Times New Roman** in the font box.

## CHANGE THE FONT SIZE

Using a large font size is very effective for letterheads, notices, and so on.

While 'Hillview House' is still selected, do the following.

Click the small arrow at the right of **12** in the next box on the toolbar – just along from the name of the font to display a list of point sizes.

Click **24** and notice that 'Hillview House' is now much larger.

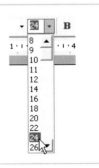

9

## USING BOLD

Making text **bold** means making it thicker and heavier, to emphasise a word or two.

Here you will make the date bold.

Select the date in the letter in the same way as you selected 'Hillview House'.

Place the **Pointer** to the left of the date and click. It becomes highlighted with a band of colour.

Click the **Bold** button – the large **B** on the toolbar just above the ruler – to make the selected text bold.

Now click anywhere on the page to remove the highlighting so that you can see the effect.

Save your work (click the **Save** button).

To remove the bold effect, if you need to, select the text as before and click the **Bold** button again. (Alternatively, click the **Undo** button.)

## USING ITALIC

Making text **italic** means making it 'lean over' to the right for emphasis but less forcibly than using bold.

Here you will make the word 'noon' italic.

Editing a Document

9

Place the **Pointer** anywhere in the word 'noon' and double-click.

'Noon' is highlighted.

Click the **I** button on the toolbar – beside the **B** button to make the selected word italic.

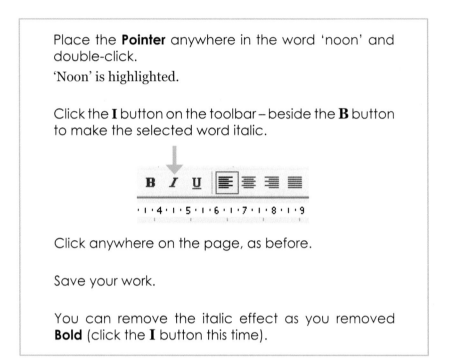

Click anywhere on the page, as before.

Save your work.

You can remove the italic effect as you removed **Bold** (click the **I** button this time).

## USING UNDERLINE

Underlining text means drawing a line under it and is another way to emphasise a word or phrase.

Here you will underline 'Saturday'.

Place the **Pointer** anywhere in the word 'Saturday' and double-click.

'Saturday' is highlighted.

Click the **U** button on the toolbar – beside the **I** button – to underline the word. (See next page).

Editing a Document

9

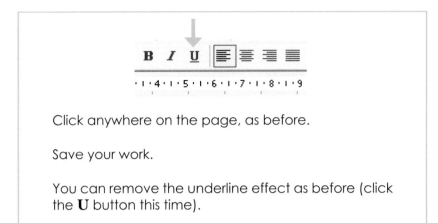

Click anywhere on the page, as before.

Save your work.

You can remove the underline effect as before (click the **U** button this time).

## SELECTING MORE THAN ONE LINE

Several lines of text can be selected at once by clicking and dragging.

To select the address and date together, do the following.

Click and hold down the mouse button anywhere in the white space to the right of the date (but on the same line, as explained before).

Drag upwards and to the left, towards the corner of the page, until the address and date are both highlighted.

Release button here

Start here

Release the mouse button.

If you don't get it right first time, try again.

## CENTRING TEXT

Centring text means moving it across to the centre of the page.

Here you will centre the address and the date that you have just selected.

The buttons just to the right of the bold, italic and underline buttons on the toolbar are used to **Align** text (align means 'line up').

Click the **Centre Align** button – arrowed in the illustration – to centre the text.

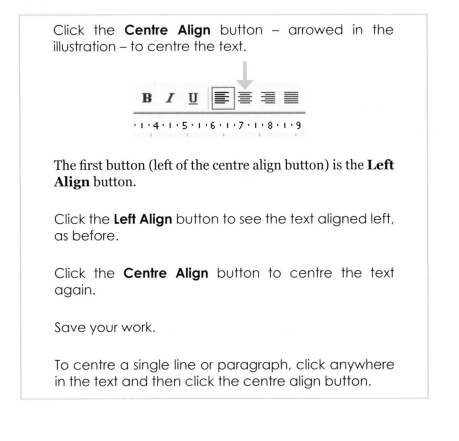

The first button (left of the centre align button) is the **Left Align** button.

Click the **Left Align** button to see the text aligned left, as before.

Click the **Centre Align** button to centre the text again.

Save your work.

To centre a single line or paragraph, click anywhere in the text and then click the centre align button.

9

## REPLACING TEXT

Imagine that the lady you are writing to is not Catherine but Kathleen.

Select the word 'Catherine' (place the pointer anywhere in the word and double-click).

Type 'Kathleen' (you do not have to click on anything first).
'Kathleen' replaces 'Catherine' in the letter.

Now change 'Saturday' to 'Sunday' in the same way.
Notice that 'Sunday' will be automatically underlined, if 'Saturday' was.

Imagine that the venue has changed from the **main entrance** to the **restaurant lobby**.

Click in the space between the words '**entrance**' and '**at**' and hold down the mouse button.

Drag to the left until both the words 'main' and 'entrance' are highlighted.

Release the mouse button.

Type 'restaurant lobby'.
What you type replaces 'main entrance' (you may have to add a space or two to tidy up).

Save your work.

# SPELLING AND GRAMMAR

Spelling is something that most people will have a little problem with, if only occasionally. Even when your spelling is good, a slip of the finger on the keyboard can introduce errors.

Perhaps you noticed some wavy red or green lines under some words as you typed them. That was Microsoft Works drawing your attention to what it regarded as either questionable spelling or questionable grammar.

**Wavy red** underlining indicates a possible spelling error.

**Wavy green** underlining indicates questionable grammar or spacing between words.

It is suggested that you to ignore grammar questions for now.

## Correcting Spelling

Do the following to check your spelling.

Click the **Spellcheck** button on the Toolbar. It has the letters **ABC** and a tick (✓) on it.

The **Spelling and Grammar** window opens.

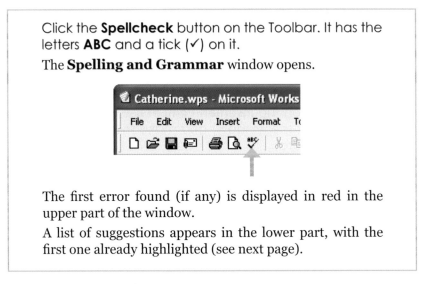

The first error found (if any) is displayed in red in the upper part of the window.

A list of suggestions appears in the lower part, with the first one already highlighted (see next page).

Editing a Document

9

## The Spellcheck Buttons

A number of buttons appear down the right-hand side of the window.

Click **Change** to replace the underlined error with the highlighted suggestion.

If the highlighted suggestion is not the right one, click the correct one to select it **before** clicking **Change**.

If none of the suggestions is appropriate, use the arrow keys to position the **Insertion Point** in the error (in the upper part of the window) and make the correction at the keyboard.

Click **Change All** to correct all occurrences of a particular error in the document.

Click **Ignore Once** or **Ignore All** to ignore just this or all occurrences of the error.

Click **Add to Dictionary** to add the marked word to Microsoft Works' dictionary. This means the word will not be questioned in future checks, e.g. local names or other unrecognised words.

When the spellcheck is complete, click **OK** in the window that appears.

**Note:** You must still read through your work for a final check. If you had typed 'meat' instead of 'meet', for example, the spellcheck would not have questioned the word because 'meat' was spelt correctly.

## CLOSING A DOCUMENT

You should save your work after you have checked the spelling or before you close it.

Click the large red **X** button to close both the document *and* the word processor.

If you forgot to save a document, a message will appear to remind you.

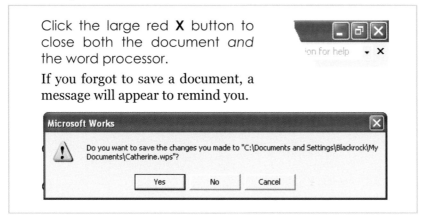

Editing a Document

9

> Click **Cancel** to return to the document without saving it.

## A NEW DOCUMENT

A new document can be opened at any time in Microsoft Works.

Do the following.

> Click the **New Document** button on the toolbar.
>
> The button resembles a small blank page.
>
>
> Remember, you can have several documents open at the same time.

In this chapter, you have learnt...

- how to find a document that you saved earlier.

- how to change the font and the font size.

- how to use bold, italic and underline.

- how to centre text on the page.

- how to check your spelling.


Do you remember...

- how to find a recently saved document?

- how to find an older document?

- where the font and font size appear on the toolbar?

- where to find the bold, italic and underline buttons?

- how to select a word, a line, more than one line?

Editing a Document

9

# CHAPTER 10
# Printing

This chapter shows you how to use your printer to print your letters and documents.

# Printing

This chapter assumes that your printer is already connected to your computer and set up so that you are ready to start printing. The document you want to print – your letter to Kathleen, for example – should be open on the screen.

You can preview a document before you print it to check how it will look on the printed page. If you don't need to preview a document, you can print it straight away by clicking the **Print** button on the toolbar.

## PREVIEWING YOUR WORK

A button on the **Toolbar** enables you to preview your document before you actually print it. It has an icon representing a sheet of paper and a magnifying glass.

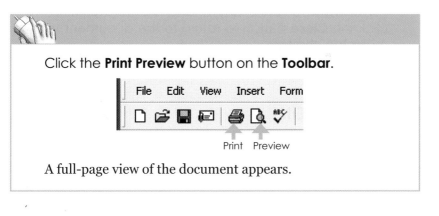

Click the **Print Preview** button on the **Toolbar**.

File    Edit    View    Insert    Form

Print    Preview

A full-page view of the document appears.

Printing

10

Move the pointer over the document. Notice that it becomes a magnifying glass with a **+** sign in it.

Enlarge

Click on the page to enlarge the document if you want to examine it more closely.

Use the scroll arrows on the right of the window to scroll through the document, if necessary.
Notice that the magnifying glass now has a – sign in it.

Reduce

Click the page again to reduce the document to its original size.

If you are happy with the preview, click the **Print** button on the **Preview** toolbar. It has an icon in the shape of a printer with paper emerging from the top.

```
'orks Word Processor
Table   Help
: Setup    Print    X Close    ?
```

If you want to make any changes before printing, click the **Close** button to return to the document to make the changes.

## THE PRINT BUTTON

Use the **Print** button on the **Microsoft Works** toolbar to print a document if you do not need to preview it.

Printing

10

Check that the printer is turned on.

Click the **Print** button to print the document.
One copy of the document is printed.

## PRINT CHOICES

If you want to print several copies or just a particular page of a large document, do the following.

Click **Print** in the **File** menu.

The Print window opens, (see next page).

Bear in mind that the **Print** window that appears on your computer may differ a little from the one in the illustration on page 154 according to the particular printer that you are using.

Printing

10

## THE PRINT WINDOW

The name of your printer appears in the **Name** box at the top of the window.

The number of copies to be printed appears in the **Number of copies** box at the right of the window.

Type the number of copies you require in the box, if you want more than one.

*Alternatively*, use the small arrows at the right of the box to enter the number of copies you want to print.

The pages to be printed appear in the **Print range** area in the left of the window. **All** is already selected so all the pages of your document will be printed.

Click **Pages from** to print only some pages of a large document.

Type the numbers of the pages to be printed in the boxes.

For example: **from 2 to 4** will print pages 2, 3 and 4; **from 4 to 4** will print only page 4.

Click the **OK** button to start printing.

Click the **Cancel** button to return to your document without printing.

Printing

10

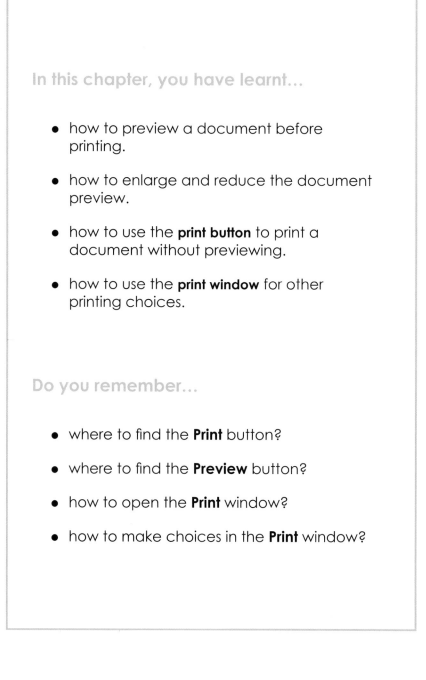

In this chapter, you have learnt...

- how to preview a document before printing.

- how to enlarge and reduce the document preview.

- how to use the **print button** to print a document without previewing.

- how to use the **print window** for other printing choices.

Do you remember...

- where to find the **Print** button?

- where to find the **Preview** button?

- how to open the **Print** window?

- how to make choices in the **Print** window?

Printing

10

# CHAPTER 11

# The Internet

This chapter introduces you to the
Internet and describes how your
computer connects to it.
It also describes how Internet pages
work and how to use them.

# The Internet

The Internet is a system that enables computers around the world to connect to each other and to share information. Anyone with a computer and an Internet connection can have access to the enormous amount of information that is available.

For most home users, the connection to the Internet is made using the ordinary house telephone line. The computer is plugged in to a telephone socket on the wall and **dials up** a remote computer to connect to the Internet.

With a dial-up connection, however, you cannot make a telephone call while you are connected to the Internet, or connect to the Internet while you are making a telephone call. If you use the Internet and email a lot, you should consider a **Broadband** connection that enables you to do both at the same time.

A broadband connection is 'always on' while your computer is turned on and there is no dial-up procedure necessary. It is also considerably faster than a dial-up connection and is to be preferred.

The Internet

11

## AN INTERNET ACCOUNT

You must have an account with an **Internet Service Provider** (ISP) before your computer can connect to the Internet.

The process of setting up an Internet account is not dealt with here. It is assumed that an Internet account has been set up for you and that you are ready to use it.

A **Username** and **Password** will have been allocated to you when your Internet account was opened. These are used when you want to connect to the Internet.

## INTERNET EXPLORER

A program called an **Internet Browser** is used to view pages on the Internet.

The most widely used browser is **Microsoft Internet Explorer**. It normally appears near the top of the **Start** menu.

If Internet Explorer is not on the **Start** menu, you will find it on the **All Programs** menu.

Click the **Internet Explorer** button to open it.

Tom

Internet
Internet Explorer

E-mail
Outlook Express

Calculator

My Documents

My Recent Documents ▶

My Pictures

My Music

The Internet Explorer window appears and displays a page of information.

The Internet

If you have a dial-up connection, there may be a connection procedure as described in the next section. There is no dial-up procedure if you have a broadband connection.

## Connecting

This section describes using a dial-up connection only.

If Internet Explorer is not set to dial up automatically, a **Dial-up Connection** window appears.

Type your user name in the **Username** box, if it is empty.

Type your password in the **Password** box, if it is empty.

Click the **Connect** button to connect to the Internet.

The Internet

11

It takes a few moments for the connection to be established.

The dial-up connection window closes when the connection has been made and the Internet Explorer window appears, if it is not displayed already.

---

**Did you notice** the two small check boxes – **Save Password** and **Connect Automatically** – in the middle of the Dial-up Connection window?

---

Do **not** place a tick in either of these boxes.

If you do, a virus or other malicious program may be able to use your computer to connect to the Internet without your knowledge. See page 168 for information on viruses and malware.

## The Internet Explorer Window

The Internet Explorer window (see next page) is similar to the many other windows you have seen already.

Click the **Maximise** button if the window does not fill the screen.

The full screen size is best for viewing most Internet pages.

The **Title Bar** at the top of the window displays the name of the page currently displayed – Blackrock Education Centre in the illustration on page 163.

The **Menu Bar** underneath displays a number of menus.

The **Button Bar**, under the menu bar, has a number of large buttons that enable you to use the program.

The **Address Bar**, under the button bar, displays the address of the page currently displayed in the main part of the window.

The Internet

11

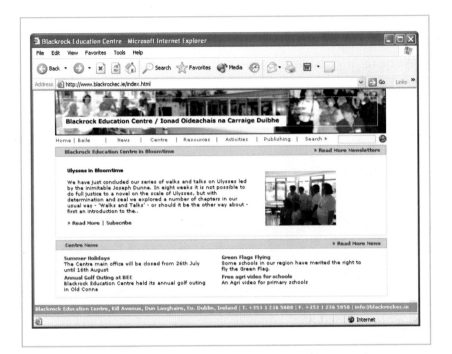

## WEB ADDRESSES

The part of the Internet that is used to display pages with text and illustrations, the pages that most people use, is called the **World Wide Web**, or **WWW** for short. Every page on the World Wide Web has its own unique **Web** address, as displayed in the address bar.

Most web page addresses have the letters **www** near the beginning. Parts of an address may be separated by a dot (full stop) or forward slash (/).

To display a page, you – or the computer – must know its address. Many web addresses can be very awkward to type. Addresses that you use often, however, can be remembered by Internet Explorer and accessed without having to retype them every time (see Chapter 12, page 184).

The Internet

11

## WEBSITES AND HOME PAGES

A **Website** is a collection of pages on the Internet. A large company may have hundreds or even thousands of pages on its website.

> Each website has its own **Home Page**. The home page is the first page that is displayed and acts as the contents page of the Website.

> From the home page, you can go to other parts of the site, depending on what information you are looking for.

The page that first appears on the screen may be any home page, depending on how Internet Explorer has been set up.

You do not have to make do with the Home Page that has been set on your computer. Internet Explorer can be set to display the home page of your choice (see Appendix, page 299).

### Reading a Web Page

Reading web pages is similar in many ways to reading pages in a newspaper. Web pages change often, however, as content and design are updated.

A web page can contain any, or all, of the following.

**Text** and **pictures**.

**Animated graphics** and **advertisements**.

**Menus** to display choices and options.

**Links** to other pages and other websites.

Because web pages change, you may return to a web page after a few days to find that it is quite different from when you last saw it.

All this can be confusing at first. You must learn to recognise what you see. You must learn to recognise what is important and what is not. You must also learn to respond to messages that may pop up from time to time.

## Links

A **link** is a piece of text or a graphic on the page with special properties. Clicking on a link displays another related page or (less often) takes you to a different part of the same page.

A piece of text that is a link – usually just a word or two – is commonly blue and underlined, like this so that you can recognise it easily.

Another way to tell a link is to move the **pointer** over it. The object is a link if the Pointer turns into a hand with a **pointing finger**.

You may also see the instruction **Click here...** to draw your attention to a link.

The Internet

11

### Menus

Menus on a web page operate in the same way as the menus you have used already.

They often appear in a menu bar across the top of the page or down the left-hand side.

When you move the **pointer** to a menu item on a web page, the menu often – but not always – appears automatically, without the need to click the mouse button.

The items in the menu act as links. Click on one to display the relevant information.

### Advertisements

As with other media, many web pages carry advertising. You will quickly learn to ignore it unless it really interests you. Clicking on an advertising link will take you to the advertiser's website and away from the page you were looking at.

An annoying form of advertising is the pop-up variety in which a new window suddenly appears on the screen without warning. Click the **Close** button in the pop-up window to close it. Some browsers, and other programs, can be set to block pop-up advertisements.

## Useful Buttons

These are some of the buttons on the Internet Explorer button bar that you will use.

The round **Back** and **Forward** buttons are at the left of the button bar. They enable you to go back to pages you have viewed earlier or forward again if you had clicked the Back button to go back.

Note that the **Back** and **Forward** buttons operate only on pages **that you have viewed**. If there are no pages to go back or forward to, the buttons will be grey and have no effect.

Use the **Stop** button if you get tired of waiting for a page to appear and you want to try something else.

The **Refresh** button fetches the latest version of the page currently displayed; it is useful for pages that may change every few seconds or minutes.

Refresh

Stop    Home

The **Home** button takes you back to the home page – the page that appears when you first open Internet Explorer.

The **History** button displays a list of pages that you have viewed, arranged by date, in a panel to the left of the window. It can be useful to return quickly to a page that you have looked at recently.

History

Click on a date or time to display a list of the pages viewed then.

Then click on the page to which you want to return.

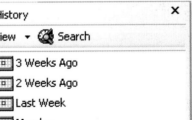

| History | ✕ |
|---|---|
| View ▾ 🔍 Search | |
| ▣ 3 Weeks Ago | |
| ▣ 2 Weeks Ago | |
| ▣ Last Week | |
| ▣ Monday | |

Click the **X** in the top right-hand corner of the History panel to close it.

Closing the panel leaves more room for the information in the main part of the window.

The Internet

## Closing and Disconnecting

Close Internet Explorer by clicking the usual red **Close** button.

The following only applies to a dial-up connection as a broadband connection does not have to be disconnected.

Closing Internet Explorer when you are using a dial-up connection does not necessarily disconnect you from the Internet. Remember, as a dial-up user you are charged while you are connected to the Internet.

While you are connected, a (very) small icon representing two computers is displayed at the right-hand end of the taskbar at the bottom of the screen.

---

**Right-click** the icon to display a small menu.

Click **Disconnect** to disconnect from the Internet.

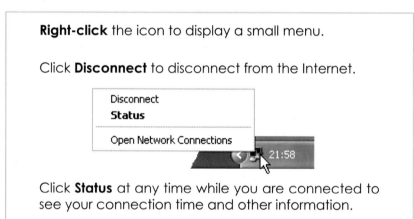

Click **Status** at any time while you are connected to see your connection time and other information.

---

## COMPUTER VIRUSES, MALWARE AND SPYWARE

Your computer may be under threat while you are connected to the Internet. If you leave the door of your house open, anyone can walk in off the street. When you are connected to the internet, a 'door' into your computer may be open to programs that 'roam' about the Internet looking for unprotected computers.

**Computer Viruses**, **Malware** and **Spyware** are malicious programs that can cause very serious problems for your computer and for you and your work.

A **Virus** can disrupt the proper working of your computer and can result in the loss of your work. **Malware** and **Spyware** (the terms are interchangeable) can obtain personal information from your computer and send it to a remote site without your knowledge. They may also force your computer to connect to unwanted (and questionable) sites on the Internet.

> **Be aware** that viruses and spyware are commonly spread via email and the Internet, particularly via email attachments.

> **Be aware also** that some viruses can come from a computer that has a friend's email address stored on it and pretend to be from that friend.

If you use email and the Internet, even if only occasionally, you should have **anti-virus** and **anti-spyware** software installed on your computer.

Many computers are now supplied with anti-virus (but not anti-spyware) software. If your computer is not protected by such programs, they can be readily obtained and installed.

> Anti-virus and anti-spyware software **must** be updated **regularly** to keep up-to-date with the latest threats. Seek advice if you are not sure about any aspect of anti-virus or anti-spyware protection.

The Internet

11

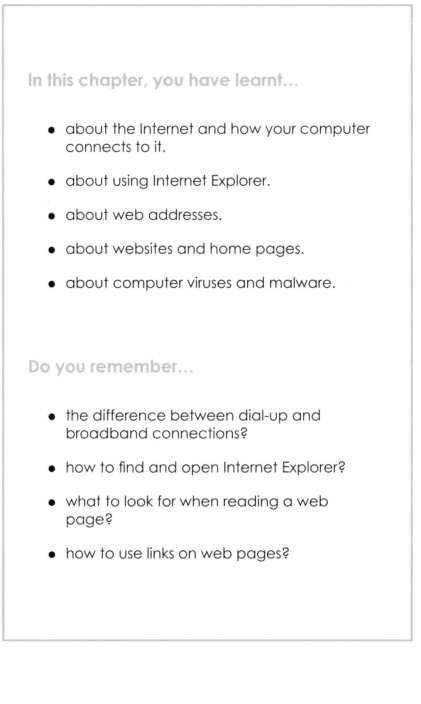

**In this chapter, you have learnt...**

- about the Internet and how your computer connects to it.

- about using Internet Explorer.

- about web addresses.

- about websites and home pages.

- about computer viruses and malware.

**Do you remember...**

- the difference between dial-up and broadband connections?

- how to find and open Internet Explorer?

- what to look for when reading a web page?

- how to use links on web pages?

The Internet

11

# CHAPTER 12
# Using the Internet

This chapter guides you in exploring some pages on the Internet.

# Using the Internet

Now, you will use some pages from the Blackrock Education Centre website for practice. Every page on the Internet has a unique address (see Chapter 11, page 163). Addresses are usually all in small letters – no capitals – and with no spaces. They begin with the characters **http://www....** However, you can omit the **http://** part and just start typing from **www.** which makes things easier.

## FINDING A PAGE

Open Internet Explorer, if it is not already open.

Find **Blackrock Education Centre** on the web as follows.

Click anywhere in the blank white space in the **Address** box.
Any text already in the box is highlighted.

Type: **www.blackrockec.ie**
What you type automatically replaces what was there already.

12

Press the **Return** key.

*Alternatively*, click the green **Go** button to the right of the Address box.

The Blackrock Education Centre home page appears.

## USING LINKS

Bear in mind that, as you do the following tasks, the main contents of the Blackrock home page will have changed since this illustration was made, just as the front page of a newspaper changes.

Using the Internet

12

Move the **pointer** over the page.

Note how it becomes a pointing finger when you move over a link or picture, for example.

Click a link to see that page appear.

Click a link on the new page to see a further page displayed.

Click the **Back** button on the toolbar to return to a previous page that you have viewed.

Click the **Forward** button to display again a page you have just come back from.

Click the **Home** button on the green Menu Bar under the main heading to return directly to the home page.

## USING MENUS

Look at the green menu bar on the Blackrock page again.

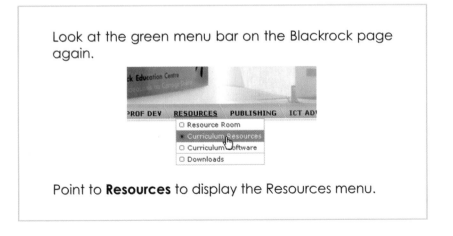

Point to **Resources** to display the Resources menu.

Click **Curriculum Resources** to display a list of resources.

Click **Make and Do...** in the list to display the **Nature Projects** page.

You will use these pages for practice.

## LOOKING AT PAGES

The **Make and Do Nature Projects** page acts as a contents page for the projects.

Notice that there is a heading at the top of the page.

An illustrated list of projects appears on the left with blue underlined links on the right.

Look at **Use Glass Jars...**, third from the top.

Click the link, **A Home For Solitary Bees**, on the right.

The Solitary Bees project page is displayed.

Notice that the Solitary Bees page also has a white menu bar across the top, under the main heading.

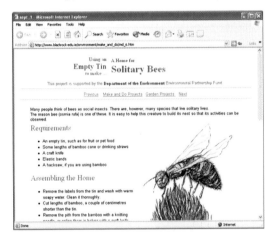

Try the following.

Click **Next** in the white menu bar to go to the next project.

Click **Previous** to go back to the page before.

Click **Make and Do Projects** to return to the contents page.

Click a link to a project and notice that the menu is also at the bottom of the page when you scroll down.

Click **Top of Page** to take you back to the top with a single click.

**12**

Click **Garden Projects** to display the Garden Projects contents page.

Notice that the small illustrations on the Garden Projects page are also links, as well as the blue underlined text above and below.

Click the link for **September** – text or illustration – to display the **Wild Flowers** project page.

Notice menus as before, this time for the different months.

Notice also the **Continue** and **Back** links where a project is spread over several pages.

Close any window that you do not need and click **Home** on the last window to return to the home page.

## SEARCHING FOR INFORMATION

How can you search for all the information that you are told is available on the Internet?

The easiest way is to use an Internet **Search Engine**, such as **Google**, which is one of the most popular and widely used.

A search engine takes your request and searches through the millions of pages available to find those relevant to what you are looking for. Then it displays the pages in order and presents them to you with, hopefully, the most relevant pages at the top of the list.

## FINDING GOOGLE

Find Google as follows.

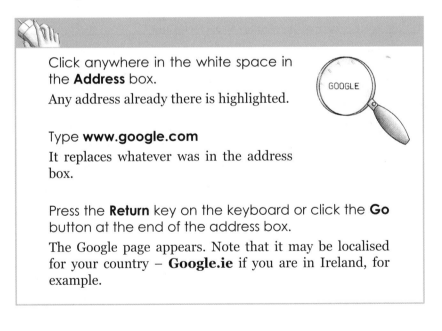

Click anywhere in the white space in the **Address** box.

Any address already there is highlighted.

Type **www.google.com**

It replaces whatever was in the address box.

Press the **Return** key on the keyboard or click the **Go** button at the end of the address box.

The Google page appears. Note that it may be localised for your country – **Google.ie** if you are in Ireland, for example.

Using the Internet

12

### The Google Page

Google's home page is clear and easy to use. How to use it is described here (the next section will then guide you in a practice search).

The cursor is flashing in a box, waiting for you to type your request. Underneath are two buttons: **Google Search** and **I'm Feeling Lucky**.

You may see two small round buttons to search the web or just pages from your own country. **Search the web** is already selected. Click the other button to narrow the search to pages from your country first.

Clicking the **Google Search** button finds the relevant pages and displays links to them, 10 at a time, with brief details. You then click a link to see that particular page.

At the bottom of each page of links is a series of page numbers and a Next button. Click the **Next** button to go to the next page of links. If you have looked at several pages, you might click a page number to return to a page that you have noted earlier.

12

Clicking **I'm Feeling Lucky** finds and displays the single page that Google thinks is the most relevant to your request. You may not always agree!

## A Google Search

How do you search with Google? Suppose that you want to find out if there is a golf club in a town that you are planning to visit.

Type 'golf' in the search box in Google (you do not need to use a capital letter).

Click the **Google Search** button.

Look at the **Results** bar near the top of the page.
About 250 million pages are found!

Results **1 - 10** of about **255,000,000** for **golf**

Searching with just one word is not very helpful!
Notice that the search box now appears at the top of the list of pages that is displayed.

Add 'club' to the search in the box, making it 'golf club'.

Click the **Search** button.
New search results appear.
Using two words reduced the search results to about 60 million pages – still too many!

Results **1 - 10** of about **73,000,000** for **golf club**

Using the Internet

12

181

Add 'Lahinch', for example, to the search, making it 'golf club lahinch'. (You do not need to use a capital 'l'.)

Click the Search button.

Using three words has narrowed down the search to about a hundred thousand pages.

Results **1 - 10** of about **110,000** for <u>golf club</u> **lahinch**.

Even now, however, the links at or near the top of the results page will most likely give you the information that you wanted (but note that sponsored commercial links sometimes appear in a shaded band at the top of the page first).

Google searched for pages with any of the separate words in the search box, so pages with golf, or club, or lahinch, are all found.

When you know the exact words to search for, place them between double quotation marks, e.g. "Lahinch Golf Club" for a more specific search.

Now only pages with all of the words in quotation marks are found.

## More Google Services

**Did you notice** the links to other services?

Click **Images** on the Google page.

Type 'lahinch' in the box.

Click **Google Search** or **Search**.

When the images appear, click on one to find more information.

Try some of the other services yourself.

Click **News link** for up-to-the minute world news (do not type anything in the box).

Click **More »** to display a range of other services. Explore!

## OTHER SEARCH ENGINES

All search engines do not search for pages in the same way. If you do not find what you are looking for with one search engine, it is a good idea to try another.

Note also that many search engines act as **portals**, or gateways, to many other facilities and services. This may make it easier to narrow your search in certain cases. Below are some other search engines for you to try out and explore.

**www.altavista.com**

**www.go2net.com**

**www.ask.com**

**www.lycos.com**

**www.excite.com**

**www.yahoo.com**

Using the Internet

12

## REMEMBERING WEB PAGES

Pages that you found interesting can be returned to at a later date without having to search for them again, especially if you have forgotten how you found them in the first place!

Internet Explorer can remember these pages as **Favorites**.

There are two ways of recording pages as Favorites: the Favorites **menu** on the menu bar or the Favorites **button** on the button bar.

### The Favorites Menu

The page that you want to remember must be on the screen. Suppose that you are looking at Blackrock Education Centre's home page and want to remember it.

Open the **Favorites** menu (click the word Favorites on the menu bar).

Click **Add to Favorites**.

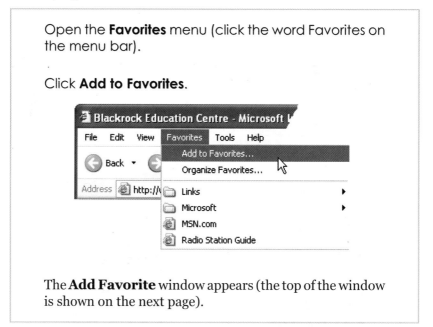

The **Add Favorite** window appears (the top of the window is shown on the next page).

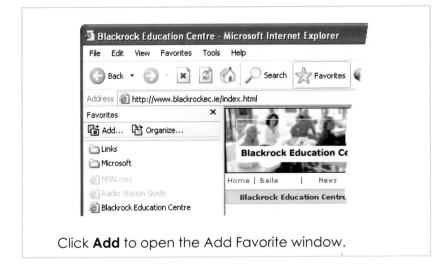

Notice the name of the page will be in the **Name** box in the window.

Click in the box to change or edit the name, if you wish.

Click the **OK** button.
The page is added to the list of Favorites.

## The Favorites Button

When you click the Favorites button on the toolbar, it opens a Favorites panel at the left of the window.

Click **Add** to open the Add Favorite window.

Using the Internet

12

Continue as described above to add the page to the list.

Click the **Close** button (the small **X**) in the top right-hand corner of the Favorites panel to close the panel when you are finished.

## Organising Favorites

Favourite websites can be saved in folders in the **Add Favorites** window (see page 185).

Click the **Create in «** button if existing folders are not displayed.

Click the **New Folder** button to create a new folder.

## Finding Favorites

To return to a web page that has been added to Favorites do the following.

Open the **Favorites** menu.

Click the required page in the list.

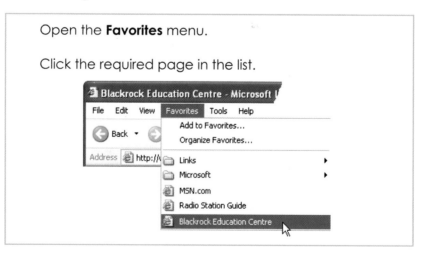

The page is found and displayed.

*Alternatively,* click the **Favorites button** and click the page that you require.

## CHILDREN ON THE WEB

Children's use of the Internet should always be controlled and supervised. You can also install a program on your computer to restrict access to material unsuitable for children.

Explore these websites for children (of all ages) for fun, learning and entertainment.

Hundreds of links to sites for children under many subject headings.

**www.linkasaurus.com**

Work by children for children.

**www.kids-space.org**

Children's version of the Yahoo site.

**www.yahooligans.yahoo.com**

'Yucky' everyday facts for children.

**www.yucky.kids.discovery.com**

Home science experiments for children.

www.bizarrelabs.com/control.htm

Education site for children and teachers.

www.skoool.ie

## Travel on the Web

Explore this sample selection of websites to search for flights or holidays. Note that you do not actually make a booking or commit yourself until the point when you are asked for your credit card details – and supply them.

aerlingus●com
www.aerlingus.com

Flybmi.com
www.flybmi.com

BRITISH AIRWAYS
www.britishairways.com

RYANAIR.COM
THE LOW FARES AIRLINE
www.ryanair.com

Some sites, such as the following, search for flights independently of any airline.

deckchair.com
www.deckchair.com

SKYscanner®
flight search engine
www.skyscanner.net

ebookers.ie
Tailormade worldwide travel
www.ebookers.com

wegolo®
time flies
www.wegolo.com

These sites specialise in last-minute deals.

**www.bargainholidays.com**

## lastminute.com

**www.lastminute.com**

This site has comprehensive information on holidays in Ireland.

**www.ireland.ie**

Use a search engine to find other airlines or companies.

## Shopping on the Web

This is a sample selection of shopping websites for you to explore.

Books, music and lots more.

## amazon.co.uk

**www.amazon.co.uk**

The catalogue shop.

**www.argos.co.uk**

Low-cost ink cartridges for your printer.

**www.bsprintcartridges.com**

Ireland's online shopping centre.

**Buy4**now

**www.buy4now.com**

Using the Internet

12

News, sport, jobs, services, etc.

**www.online.ie**

Supermarket shopping from home.

**www.superquinn.com**

Groceries, wines and more.

**TESCO**
IRELAND

**www.tesco.com**

Be aware of VAT, delivery or other charges that may be payable. This is particularly important if you are ordering from a company based outside the country.

## CREDIT CARD SECURITY

While millions of safe credit card transactions are conducted on the Internet every day, you should note the following.

Only supply your credit card details to a company or organisation that you know to be reputable.

The page on which you supply your credit card details should be a **secure** page. You may see a message drawing your attention to this (click **OK** to proceed).

Using the Internet

The address of a secure page (near the top of the window) will begin with **https** instead of just **http**.

A small closed **lock** also appears in the bottom right-hand corner of the window.

## CLOSING AND DISCONNECTING

Closing and disconnecting is described in Chapter 11, Page 168.

Look back to refresh your memory, if necessary.

Using the Internet

12

In this chapter, you have learnt...

- how to use an Internet address to find a page.

- how to use links on a page.

- how to use menus on a page.

- how to use Google to search for information.

Do you remember...

- how to type an Internet address?

- how to recognise and use links on a page?

- how to find Google?

- how using more than one word narrows a Google search?

- how to use Favorites to remember pages?

Using the Internet

12

# CHAPTER 13

# Email

This chapter tells you about email.
It describes the Outlook Express email
program and shows you how to use it.

# Email

To use email, you must have an Internet connection and an account with an Internet Service Provider, as described in Chapter 11. Then an email message written on your computer can be sent almost instantly and will cost much less than the price of a postage stamp. You can attach a copy of a document you have already prepared on the computer or a photograph from your digital camera to an email message.

## HOW DOES EMAIL WORK?

Email is the computer equivalent of the Post Office Box system, where you have to go to the Post Office, open your P.O. Box and look inside to see if there is any mail.

Email

195

13

When an email message is sent, it does not go directly to the recipient's computer, which is most probably turned off most of the time anyway.

Instead, it goes to the electronic equivalent of the recipient's local post office.

To check for email, your computer contacts your electronic Post Office. If it finds any email for you, it collects it and brings it back to your computer.

So, although email can be almost instantaneous in going from one side of the world to another, how long it takes for you to see it depends on how often you check your email.

An **email address**, and a separate **username** and **password** to use with it, may have been allocated to you when your Internet account was opened.

Your **email address** is what people use to send messages to you by email, just as you need a street address so that people can send you letters by post. You will recognise an email address because it always has an 'at' (**@**) symbol in it.

Your **username** is a unique name that identifies you, usually a version of your name, such as **tom** or **tmacm**. A short username is easier to type and to remember.

Your **password**, like a bank **PIN** number, ensures that no one else can have access to your email.

## OUTLOOK EXPRESS

**Outlook Express** is the program that most people use for email. It normally appears near the top of the **Start** menu.

Email

13

Click the **E-mail/Outlook Express** button to open it.

If Outlook Express is not on the **Start** menu, you will find it in the **All Programs** menu.

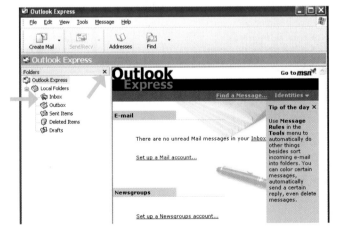

When you open Outlook Express, it connects to the Internet in the same way as Internet Explorer. There may be a connection procedure if you use a dial-up connection. Look back at Chapter 11, page 161) to refresh your memory if necessary.

## The Outlook Express Window

Information about Outlook Express is displayed when you open it for the first time.

E m a i l

13

To display the **Inbox**, where you will work most, do the following.

Click **Inbox** in the **Folders** panel at the left of the window. (See illustration on previous page).

Then click the small **Close** button (arrowed) to leave more space in the Inbox window.

## The Inbox

The **Title Bar** at the top of the window tells you that you are looking at the **Inbox** – email that has been received.

Immediately underneath the title bar is the **Menu Bar** with its menus.

The **Button Bar** under the menu bar contains a number of large buttons that enable you to use the program.

The thick grey bar under the button bar reminds you that what is displayed here is the **Inbox**.

The panel in the centre of the window displays details of messages that have been received. A welcome message appears there now. (Arrowed on previous page).

The panel underneath displays the message currently selected in the panel above. Notice that only brief details of the messages appear in the centre panel.

To read a message, you must click on it in the upper panel to see it displayed below.

The **Status Bar** at the bottom of the window displays other information.

Remember, you can resize, or even maximise this and other windows, if necessary.

## PREPARING AN EMAIL

Send an email to yourself (just as you can post a letter to yourself) in order to practise.

> Click the **Create Mail** button at the left of the **Button Bar.**
>
> The **New Message** window opens, (see next page).
>
> Notice that your own details may be automatically entered in the **From** box near the top of the window.
>
> For this exercise, type your own email address in the **To** box (the cursor is already flashing there).
>
> Click in the **Subject** box and type a brief subject heading (what the email is about, e.g. 'Test Email').

Email

13

It is important to type a subject heading when you are sending an email. It appears in the recipient's Inbox to indicate what the message is about. A message with a blank subject heading can be unwelcome and may be treated with suspicion.

Click anywhere in the large panel in the lower part of the window and type your message.

Don't forget to put your name at the end, as you would with any message or letter.

## Sending Your Email

All you need to do is to click a button.

Click the **Send** button at the left of the button bar (arrowed on next page).

Your email is sent and the Create Mail window closes.

Email

13

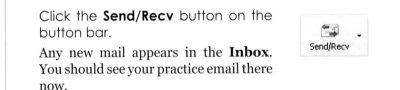

## Checking for Mail

Your computer may be set up to check for mail every time you open **Outlook Express**.

To check for new mail at any time after opening Outlook Express, do the following.

> Click the **Send/Recv** button on the button bar.
>
> Any new mail appears in the **Inbox**. You should see your practice email there now.

Notice that messages in the Inbox have an icon to the left in the form of an envelope.

The envelope indicates whether or not you have clicked on the message to read it. A **closed envelope** shows that you have not read that particular message. An **opened envelope** shows that the particular message has been read.

## Replying to a Message

You will want to reply to many of the email messages you receive.

Email

13

Click the message (in the upper part of the window) that you want to reply to, in order to select it.

Click the **Reply** button on the button bar.
A new window, similar to the Create Mail window, opens.

Notice the following.

Your own details may have already been inserted in the **From** box.

The details of the person to whom you are replying have already been inserted in the **To** box.

The subject heading of the original email has also been inserted in the **Subject** box, prefaced by **Re:** (about).

The cursor is flashing in the main part of the window, ready for you to start typing.

The original message – the one you are replying to – may appear underneath.

Email

13

## Write and Send Your Reply

Using the keyboard, type your reply.

If necessary, click the **Spelling** button to check your spelling.

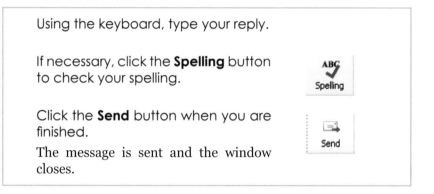

Click the **Send** button when you are finished.

The message is sent and the window closes.

## Forwarding a Message

Occasionally, you may want to send – or **Forward** – someone a copy of a message that you have received. The process of forwarding a message is very similar to replying to a message.

Proceed as follows.

Click the **Forward** button on the button bar.

A window opens with a copy of the original message.

Email

13

Type the address of the person to whom you are forwarding the message in the **To** box (the cursor is already flashing there for you).

Click and type a brief message above the message being forwarded (optional).

Click the **Send** button.

## Printing a Message

You can easily print out a copy of an email message.

Check that your printer is turned on.

Click the message that you want to print in the upper part of the Inbox, to display it in the lower part.

Click the **Print** button on the button bar.

Print

## Deleting a Message

Unwanted messages can be deleted as follows.

Click the message in the upper part of the Inbox that you want to delete.

Click the **Delete** button on the button bar.

Delete

Email

13

## Attaching a File

A copy of a document, photograph or other file already on your computer can be sent with – or **attached** *to* – a new email message or to one that you are replying to or forwarding.

Be aware, however, that attaching a large document or picture (see below) can slow down the sending and receiving process, especially when you are using a dial-up connection.

When the new message is ready to be sent, proceed as follows.

Click the **Attach** button on the toolbar. It has a paper clip on it.

Attach

The Insert Attachment window appears.

The **Look in** box at the top of the window tells you that you are looking in the **My Documents** folder.

Click the item that you want to attach – in this example the **Catherine** file – to select it.

Use the scroll arrows at the right of the window, if necessary, to find the file you need.

Email

13

Click the **Attach** button at the bottom right-hand corner of the window to attach the selected document to your email message.

The **Insert Attachment** window closes and you are returned to your email message.

Notice that details of the attached document now appear in a new box in the message window.

| From: | tmacm@blackrock-edu.ie (tmacm) |
|---|---|
| To: | ethnab@netlink.ie |
| Cc: | |
| Subject: | Letter to Catherine |
| Attach: | Catherine.doc (19.5 KB) |

| Arial | 10 | B _I_ |

Repeat the process outlined above if you want to attach another file.

## Attaching a Picture

If your pictures are stored in the **My Pictures** folder, proceed as if you were attaching a document until the **Insert Attachment** window appears. Then...

Double-click the **My Pictures** folder to open it.

Click the picture that you want to attach, to select it (see next page).

Click the **Attach** button at the bottom right-hand corner of the window to attach the selected picture to your email message.

**Insert Attachment**

Look in: My Pictures

House | Sample Pictures

File name: | Attach
Files of type: All Files (*.*) | Cancel
☐ Make Shortcut to this file

Note that only a copy of a document or picture is attached. The original remains on your computer. Note also that pictures from you digital camera can be edited in an image-editing program to reduce the time it takes to send and receive them.

## Opening Email Attachments

When you receive an attachment with an email message, it may be represented by a **paper clip** symbol in the corner of the message window or by a link – the name of the attachment in blue, underlined – at the bottom of the message.

Click the '**paper clip**' or the **link** under the message to open the attachment.

Beware of opening strange email attachments, however. See the Virus and Malware section in Chapter 11, page 168. You should never open an email attachment that you are unsure of, even if it appears to come from someone you know. You should check with the sender first to see if it is genuine.

VIRUS ALERT!

Email

13

Delete any suspect messages or attachments **without opening them**.

## Message Folders

Outlook Express organises your messages in a number of folders.

Click the **Inbox** button on the grey bar to display a list of those folders.

Notice that **Inbox** is highlighted in the list that appears because it is the folder that is currently open.

The **Outbox** folder contains messages (if any) that have not yet been sent.

The **Sent Items** folder stores copies of messages that you have sent. You can look here to refresh your memory of messages you sent earlier.

The **Deleted Items** folder stores items that have been deleted from the list.

The **Drafts** folder stores messages that you are working on until you are ready to send them.

## Selecting a Folder

Click a folder in the list to select it. The contents of the folder are displayed and its name now appears in the title bar and on the button on the grey bar.

Before you close Outlook Express, click the button on the grey bar again.

Then click **Inbox** to ensure that the Inbox is displayed when you next open the program.

Note that you can keep the list of folders open if you click the 'pin' (arrowed) at the top of the list. The pin then becomes an **X** that you can click to close the list.

As you do not need to refer to folders other than the Inbox often, keeping the list closed gives more room in the window for your messages.

## Closing and Disconnecting

Closing and disconnecting is described in Chapter 11, page 168.

Look back to refresh your memory if necessary.

Email

13

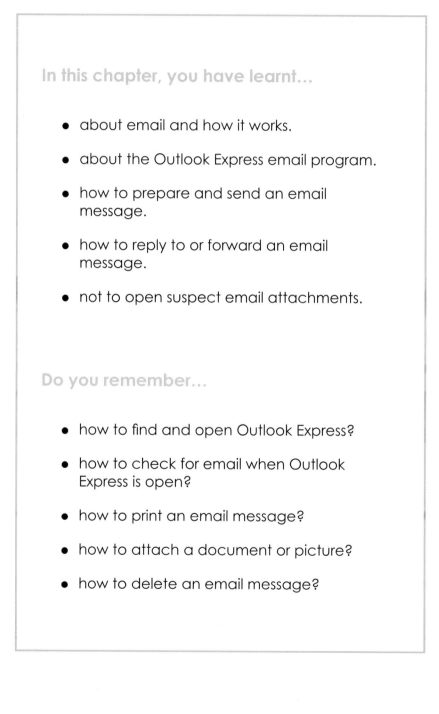

In this chapter, you have learnt...

- about email and how it works.

- about the Outlook Express email program.

- how to prepare and send an email message.

- how to reply to or forward an email message.

- not to open suspect email attachments.

Do you remember...

- how to find and open Outlook Express?

- how to check for email when Outlook Express is open?

- how to print an email message?

- how to attach a document or picture?

- how to delete an email message?

Email

13

## CHAPTER 14

# Web Mail

This chapter explains the difference between ordinary email and web mail.
It describes a popular web mail program and shows you how to use it.

# Web Mail

Web mail uses an Internet browser, such as **Internet Explorer**, instead of an email program, such as **Outlook Express**. An advantage of web mail is that you can access your email from any computer with an Internet connection. If you are away from home, you can drop in to a friend's house or go to an Internet cafe. You can reply to messages, send new ones and so on – just as you would if you were at home.

The major difference, compared with using **Outlook Express**, as described in Chapter 13, is that all your email is stored on the **Email provider's** computer, not on your own computer or whatever computer that you happen to be using at the time.

This means that you cannot search through your email messages without being connected to the Internet. Also, web mail providers only allow you a certain amount of storage that can be filled up quickly if you use email a lot and you do not like to delete many messages.

Web Mail

14

## HOTMAIL

**Hotmail** is a popular web mail service that has the same appearance on all computers. As the basic operations are the same for most web mail services, you should be able to relate what is described in this chapter to your own service, if you are not using Hotmail.

The process of setting up a Hotmail account is not described here. It is assumed that this has been done for you and that you have been allocated a **Username** and **Password** as described in Chapter 11.

## Finding Hotmail

Hotmail is accessed through a page on the Internet.

Proceed as follows.

Connect to the Internet (if you do not have a broadband connection).

Open **Internet Explorer**, if it is not already open.

Type the Hotmail address in the address box: **www.hotmail.com**.

Press the **Return** key or click the **Go** button at the right of the address box.

The Hotmail page appears (see next page).

Look for the **Sign In to Hotmail** panel, which should appear prominently on the page.

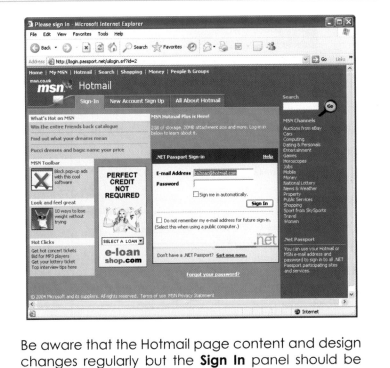

Be aware that the Hotmail page content and design changes regularly but the **Sign In** panel should be easy to see.

## Signing In

The **Sign In** panel (see next page) has two boxes: one for your email address and one for your password.

Your **Email address** may appear automatically in the email address box.

If not, click in the box and type it in.

Click in the **Password** box and type your password.

Web Mail

**.NET Passport Sign-in**                    Help

E-mail Address

Password

☐ Sign me in automatically.

[ Sign In ]

☐ Do not remember my e-mail address for future sign-in.
(Select this when using a public computer.)

Microsoft
.net

Don't have a .NET Passport? **Get one now.**

When you are using a computer other than your own, you should click on **Do not remember my e-mail address...** to place a tick in the box. This will prevent other users of that computer from seeing – and possibly using – your email account.

Click the **Sign In** button.

Click **OK** or **Yes** if **Security Alert** messages appear.

**Security Alert**                        ☒

You are about to view pages over a secure connection.

Any information you exchange with this site cannot be viewed by anyone else on the Web.

☐ In the future, do not show this warning

[ OK ]  [ More Info ]

There is usually no cause for alarm.

## Wrong Password

It's easy to make a mistake when you are typing in your password. If this happens, a large message window appears, most of which you can safely ignore. Look for the part of the message window, shown below.

**E-mail Address** *ta2mac@hotmail.com*

**Password**

☐ Sign me in automatically.

**Continue**

☐ Do not remember my e-mail address for future sign-in. (Select this when using a public computer.)

Type in your password again in the box.

Click the **Continue** button.

Click **Do not remember…**, if necessary.

## Finding Your Mail

After signing in, another page will appear with a lot of information and advertisements.

Look at the part of the window shown here. A list of received messages will appear under the **Today** tab, as in the illustration.

Web Mail

14

To enlarge the lower part of the window and display an expanded list of your messages, do one of the following.

> Click the **Mail** tab.
>
> *Alternatively,* Click on **My Messages**.

Email that has been received is stored in the **Inbox** folder. The contents of the Inbox are what is displayed on your screen now.

## Reading Your Mail

The Inbox window is shown here with some advertising content removed for clarity.

Only the message headings – sender, subject, and so on – are shown in the list.

14

Click on the sender's name, in the **From** column, to display the actual message.

You can also click on a message under the **Today** tab on the previous screen to display it.

Notice the **Button Bar** (arrowed on the previous page) over the list of messages, we will refer to later.

Click **Inbox** at the top-right of the message to return to the Inbox.

## A PRACTICE EMAIL

Before going any further, prepare and send an email to yourself to practise.

Click the **New** button to open the **New Message** window.

Notice that a **New** button also appears under the **Today** tab when you sign in. It is not necessary to go to the inbox if you only want to send an email.

Web Mail

14

## Preparing a New Message

The main part of the new message window is shown here.

Type your own email address in the **To** box at the top (the cursor is already flashing there).

Leave the **Cc** and **Bcc** boxes empty.

Click in the **Subject** box and type a brief subject heading (what the email is about).

For this exercise type **Practice Email**.

Click anywhere in the large panel in the lower part of the window and type your message. A few words will suffice for the purpose of this exercise.

## SENDING YOUR EMAIL

All you need to do is to click a button.

Click the **Send** button at the left of the Bar just above the **To** box.

Your email is sent and the **New Message** window closes. A message appears confirming that the message has been sent.

Click **Return to Inbox** to continue.

## Checking for Mail

New email appears automatically in the inbox when you open Hotmail.

You can check for mail that may have come in after you opened Hotmail at any time by clicking **Inbox** at the left of the messages.

Notice that messages in the inbox have an icon at the left in the form of an envelope.

The **envelope** indicates whether or not you have clicked on the message to read it.

A **closed envelope** shows that you have not read that particular message. An **open envelope** shows that the particular message has been read.

Web Mail

## Replying to a Message

You will want to reply to many of the email messages you receive.

Display the message to which you want to reply.

Click the **Reply** button on the button bar.

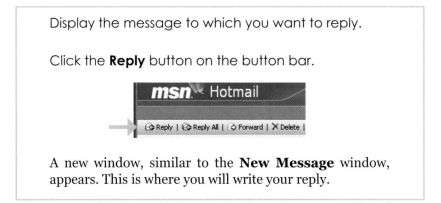

A new window, similar to the **New Message** window, appears. This is where you will write your reply.

Notice the following.

The email address of the person to whom you are replying has already been inserted in the **To** box.

The subject heading of the original email has also been inserted in the **Subject** box, prefaced by **Re:** (about).

The cursor is flashing in the main part of the window below, ready for you to start typing.

Web Mail

14

The original message – the one you are replying to – appears underneath (not shown in the illustration).

## Write and Send Your Reply

Using the keyboard, type your reply.

You do not have to click on anything first.

Click the **Send** button at the left of the button bar when you are finished.

The message is sent and a confirmation message appears, as before.

## Forwarding a Message

Occasionally, you may want to send – or **Forward** – someone a copy of a message that you have received. The process is very similar to replying to a message.

Click the **Forward** button on the button bar.

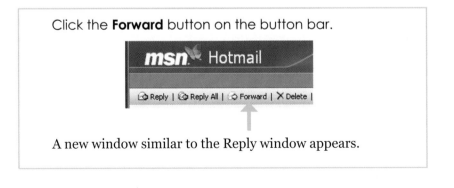

A new window similar to the Reply window appears.

Web Mail

Type the address of the person you are forwarding the message to in the **To** box (the cursor is already flashing there for you).

Click and type a brief message above the message being forwarded (optional).

Click the **Send** button.

A confirmation message appears, as before.

## Printing a Message

If you want to print a message, you should use the special printable form of the message that excludes advertisements and other material.

Proceed as follows.

Check that your printer is turned on.

Display the message that you want to print.

Click the **Print View** button at the right-hand end of the button bar.

A new window appears with the message in printable format.

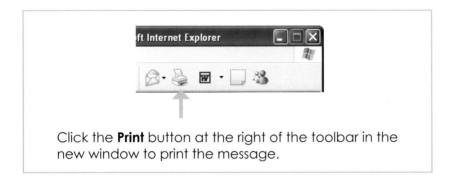

Click the **Print** button at the right of the toolbar in the new window to print the message.

## Deleting a Message

Unwanted messages can be deleted as follows.

Display the message that you want to delete.

Click the **Delete** button on the button bar.

If you are looking at the list of messages in the **Inbox** or under the **Today** tab, the procedure is a little different.

You will have noticed that there is a small box next to the envelope icon at the left of each message.

Click the box of the message that you want to delete (this places a tick in it).

Web Mail

225

> Click the **Delete** button on the button bar to delete the message.
>
> If you placed a tick in a box by mistake, click the box again to remove the tick.

## Sending an Existing File

A copy of a document, photograph or other file already on your computer can be sent with – or **Attached to** – a new email message, or to one that you are replying to or forwarding.

When the message is ready to be sent, proceed as follows.

> Click the **Attach** button on the button bar. It has a 'paper clip' on it.
>
>
>
> A small menu appears.
>
> Click **File** in the menu.
>
> A new page appears, asking you to find the file that you want to send with your email.

## Finding a File to Attach

When the **Attach File** page appears, follow these steps.

1    Click the **Browse** button to the right of the **Find File** box to search for the file to attach.

The **Choose File** window appears.

Look at the **Look in** box at the top of the window to see where the computer is looking for the file.

2    If you see **My Documents** in the Look in box, you will see the items in the My Documents folder displayed in the main part of the window.

Go to step 6.

Web Mail

14

**3** If **My Documents** does not appear in the Look in window, click the large **My Documents** button at the left of the window and go to step 6.

**4** If the file you want to attach is on the **Desktop**, click the large **Desktop** button at the left of the window.

**Desktop** now appears in the Look in box and you will see the items on the desktop displayed in the main part of the window.

Go to step 6.

**5** If the **file** you want to attach is in another folder in the **My Documents** folder, double-click the folder, **Letters**, for example.

The folder you double-clicked now appears in the Look in box. The contents of the folder are displayed in the main part of the window.

**6** Double-click the file in the main part of the window that you want to attach.

The **Attach File** page returns.

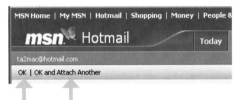

**7** Click the small **OK** button at the left of the button bar or **OK and Attach Another** if you want to attach another file.

You are returned to your email and details of the attachment(s) appear just above the main message box.

## ATTACHING A PICTURE – 1

You can attach a picture to an email message by clicking either **Pictures** or **File** in the **Attach** menu. Clicking **Pictures** enables you to edit the picture first, if necessary, while clicking **File** omits the editing steps.

To use the editing method, proceed as follows.

Click the **Attach** button on the button bar. It has a 'paper clip' on it.

A small menu appears.

Web Mail

14

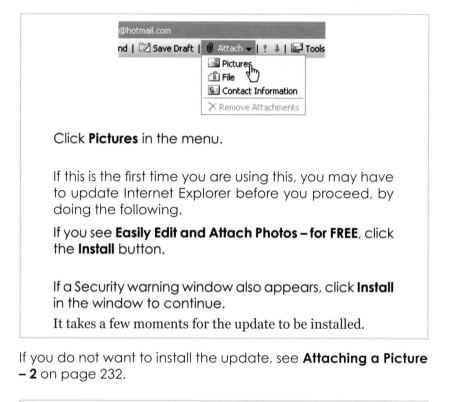

Click **Pictures** in the menu.

If this is the first time you are using this, you may have to update Internet Explorer before you proceed, by doing the following.

If you see **Easily Edit and Attach Photos – for FREE**, click the **Install** button.

If a Security warning window also appears, click **Install** in the window to continue.

It takes a few moments for the update to be installed.

If you do not want to install the update, see **Attaching a Picture – 2** on page 232.

When the update is installed, a list of folders appears at the left, with the **My Pictures** folder already highlighted.

If your pictures are in another folder, click on that folder to select it.

The pictures in the folder are displayed on the right.

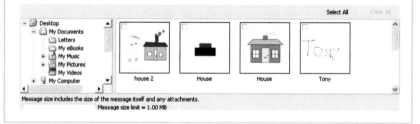

Use the scroll arrows at the right of the panel to scroll through them, if necessary.

Click on the picture, or pictures, that you want to attach.

This places a tick mark in the small box at the top left of each picture, to show that it has been selected.

Click on the picture again to remove the tick, if you change your mind.

Click the **Attach Files** button at the top right to attach the selected picture(s) to the email message.

It takes a few moments for the picture(s) to be attached.

You are then returned to your email and details of the attachment(s) appear just above the main message box.

## Editing a Picture

**Did you notice** the buttons that appear underneath a picture as you move the pointer over it?

Click to edit title

Web Mail

14

Click either of the two circular buttons to rotate the picture, to turn it the right way up, for example, if you rotated your digital camera when taking the picture.

Click **Click to edit title** to change the title or to give the picture a new title.

Click the button with the pencil or click the **Edit Photos** button above and to the right of the pictures to make other adjustments.

The picture appears with a button bar above it. Point to a button to see what it does.

Click the buttons as required, to increase or decrease the brightness of the picture, for example.

Click **Attach Photos** to attach the pictures when you have finished or **View Thumbnails** to return to all the pictures.

## Attaching a Picture – 2

If you do not want to use the **Attach Picture** method described above, proceed as if you were attaching a file (as described on page 227) until **My Documents** appears in the **Look in box**.

Then (if your pictures are stored in the **My Pictures** folder), do the following.

Double-click the **My Pictures** folder (arrowed on next page) to open it.

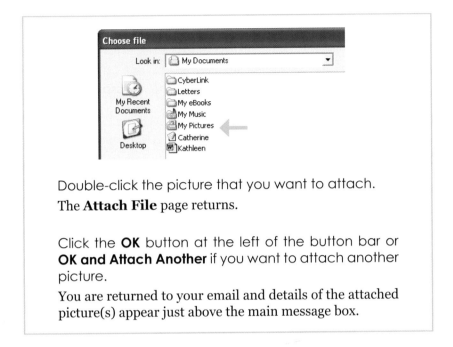

Double-click the picture that you want to attach.
The **Attach File** page returns.

Click the **OK** button at the left of the button bar or
**OK and Attach Another** if you want to attach another
picture.

You are returned to your email and details of the attached
picture(s) appear just above the main message box.

Note that only a copy of the file or picture is attached. The
original remains on your computer.

Sending (and receiving) a large file or picture can take a
long time if you have a dial-up connection. However, an
image-editing program can be used to reduce the time for
sending and receiving pictures.

## Sending the Email

Click the **Send** button at the left of the button bar to
send the email with the attached file(s).

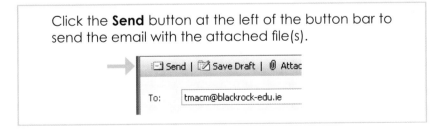

Web Mail

14

A message appears confirming that the email has been sent.

Click **Return to Inbox** (just under the message) to continue.

## Signing Out

When you have attended to your email, you can **Sign Out** from Hotmail if you want to continue using the Internet for something else.

Click the **Sign Out** button near the top of the window, shown above the **Mail** tab in the illustration. (Advertising has been removed here for clarity.)

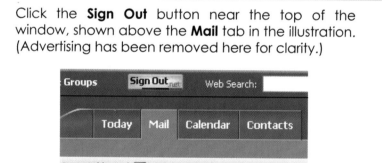

Signing out closes your Hotmail connection but leaves you connected to the Internet. You will see the Microsoft Network (MSN) page displayed.

*Alternatively*, click the **Close** button to close the window if you do not want to continue using the Internet.

Remember, however, that you may still have to disconnect from the Internet (see Chapter 11, page 168).

Web Mail

14

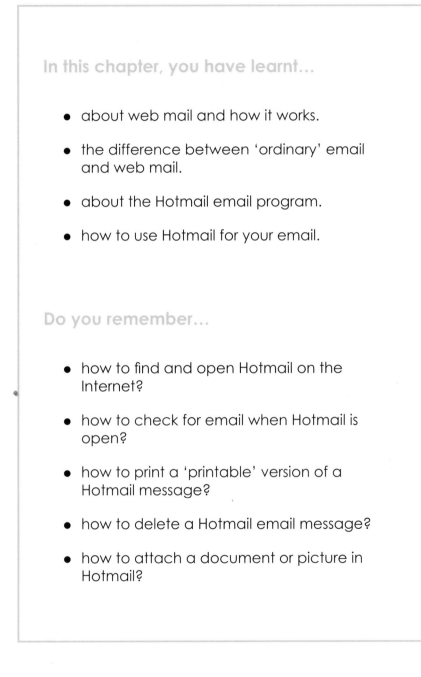

In this chapter, you have learnt...

- about web mail and how it works.

- the difference between 'ordinary' email and web mail.

- about the Hotmail email program.

- how to use Hotmail for your email.


Do you remember...

- how to find and open Hotmail on the Internet?

- how to check for email when Hotmail is open?

- how to print a 'printable' version of a Hotmail message?

- how to delete a Hotmail email message?

- how to attach a document or picture in Hotmail?

Web Mail

14

# CHAPTER 15
# Using Folders

This chapter shows you how to file and organise your work and help keep your desktop tidy.

# Using Folders

Look into almost any office and one of the pieces of office furniture that you will see is a filing cabinet. Open the filing cabinet and, inside, you will find numerous **folders**, each one neatly labelled with the name of the subject or topic of the documents it contains. When documents are filed away, they are placed in the correct folder from which they can be quickly and easily retrieved later when required.

The **Hard Disk** in your computer is the electronic equivalent of the office filing cabinet. It is where all the work that you save is stored.

All the programs the computer uses and all the programs that you yourself use are also stored there.

The calculator, Solitaire, word processor, your letter to Catherine, the picture of the house that you drew, are all stored on the hard disk.

Like the filing cabinet in the office, programs and documents are stored in labelled **folders** on the hard disk.

When you saved files earlier, they were automatically saved in the **My Documents** folder.

The My Documents folder – and other folders – can also act as a drawer in which more folders can be stored.

15

## CREATING FOLDERS

Now you will learn how to create new folders and to save documents in them.

To open the **My Documents** folder, do the following.

Click the **Start** button.

The Start menu appears.

Click **My Documents** located on the right of the menu.

The My Documents window opens.

## My Documents

The contents of the My Documents folder are displayed in the right of the My Documents window.

A panel on the left displays information that we shall come to later.

You will see the letter to Catherine that you saved there already. Notice that its icon shows that it is a Microsoft Works document.

If necessary, use the scroll buttons at the right of the window to view all the contents of the My Documents folder.

Tiles View

As well as containing files and documents, a folder can also have other folders within it, such as the **My Pictures** and other folders shown here.

## Different Views

Open the **View** menu to see how the contents of a folder can be displayed in different ways. Click on the different views, described below, to see them.

Using Folders

15

**Tiles View** shows the files and folders arranged in alphabetical order. (See illustration on previous page).

**Thumbnails View** displays the files as small pictures. This view is useful for pictures and graphics.

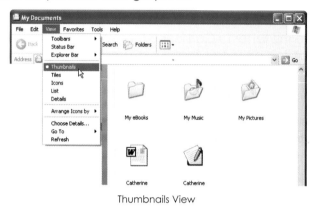
Thumbnails View

**Icons View** displays the files and folders as icons. It is the view used by many people.

Icons View

**List View** shows the files and folders in a list with small icons on the left. People who work with a lot of files like to use this view because more files can be shown in the same space.

List View

**Details View** is similar to **List View** but information about each item is also displayed.

Select the view you prefer. The next time you open that folder, the view that you have selected will be used.

# ORGANISING YOUR WORK

The **My Documents** folder will soon become cluttered if all your work is saved there, with everything in the same folder.

The solution is to save your work in different folders. There can be a folder for **Letters**, a folder for **Family documents**, a folder for **Work**, and so on.

## A New Folder

Now, you will make a new folder for letters in the My Documents folder.

Open the **My Documents** folder, if it is not already open.

Click **Make a New Folder** in the **File and Folder Tasks** panel at the left of the My Documents window.

Using Folders

15

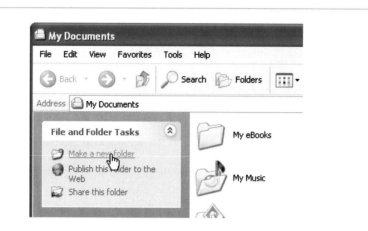

A new folder appears in the main part of the window on the right, with the title **New Folder**, already highlighted.

Using the keyboard, type **Letters** (you do not have to use the mouse or click on anything first).

Letters replaces **New Folder** as the title of the folder.

Click anywhere in the window to finish, or press the **Return** key.

## Sorting Files and Folders

When you created the new folder, it appeared at the bottom of the list in the window. You might like to arrange the contents of the window in a more convenient way.

Files and Folders can be arranged by name – in alphabetical order – or in other ways.

Open the **View** menu.

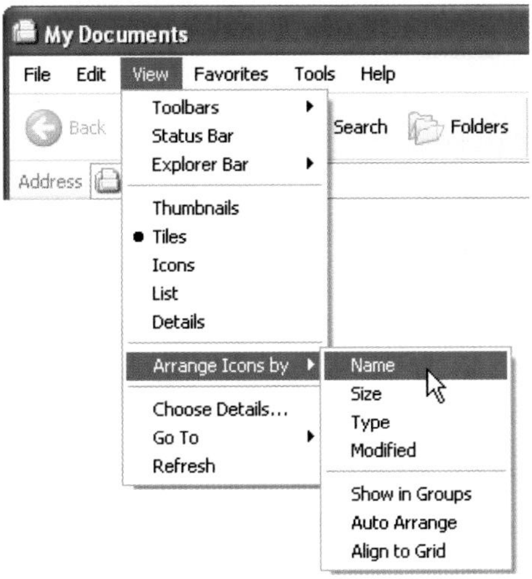

Point to **Arrange Icons by**.

A new menu appears.

Click **Name** to arrange the files and folders in alphabetical order.

Notice that the folders are now arranged together at the top of the list while individual files are listed below them.

## Renaming a File or Folder

Before proceeding, rename the letter to Catherine which, you will remember, became a letter to **Kathleen**.

**Right-click** the **Catherine** file in the My Documents window.

A menu appears.

Using Folders

15

Catherine.wps
Microsoft ~~Works Word Processor~~
10 KB

| |
|---|
| **Open** |
| New |
| Open With |
| Send To |
| Cut |
| Copy |
| Create Shortcut |
| Delete |
| Rename |

Click **Rename**, near the bottom of the menu.
The title of the file is highlighted.

Go to the keyboard and type **Kathleen**.
Kathleen replaces Catherine as the title of the file.

Click anywhere in the window to finish or press the **Return** key.
This procedure can also be used to rename a folder.

## Moving a File or Folder

Now that you have a special folder for letters, you can move the letter to Kathleen into it. Moving a file is just a matter of dragging it to its new location.

Proceed as follows.

Drag the **Kathleen** file onto the **Letters** folder.

A faint copy of the file moving appears as you drag.

The Letters folder is highlighted – darkens – when the Kathleen file is dragged over it.

Release the mouse button when the **Letters** folder is highlighted. The file now disappears into the folder.

If the folder is not highlighted when you release the button, the file will not go into the folder. Instead, it will appear beside the folder or on top of it. If that happens, try again.

## A NEW LETTER

To practise what you have learnt, you will now write a letter to Kathleen thanking her for meeting you. You will then save it in the new **Letters** folder.

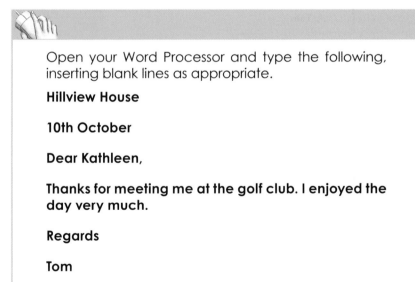

Open your Word Processor and type the following, inserting blank lines as appropriate.

**Hillview House**

**10th October**

**Dear Kathleen,**

**Thanks for meeting me at the golf club. I enjoyed the day very much.**

**Regards**

**Tom**

Using Folders

15

## Saving in a New Folder

To save your letter, proceed as follows.

Click the **Save** button on the toolbar at the top of the window.

The **Save As** window appears.

Type the title 'Kathleen - Thanks' in the **File name** box at the bottom of the window.

| File name: | Kathleen - Thanks |
| --- | --- |

(Look back at Chapter 8, page 123, to refresh you memory if necessary.)

**Double-click** the **Letters** folder to open it.

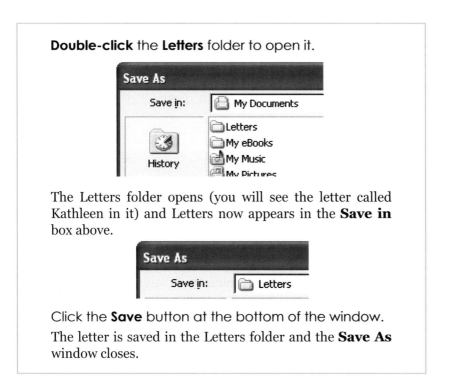

The Letters folder opens (you will see the letter called Kathleen in it) and Letters now appears in the **Save in** box above.

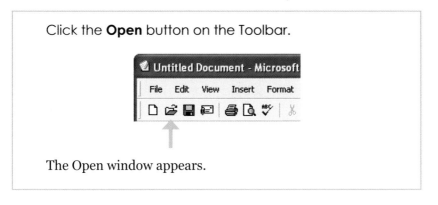

Click the **Save** button at the bottom of the window.

The letter is saved in the Letters folder and the **Save As** window closes.

## Reopening a Document

If the document in the **Letters** folder that you want to open is not on the list of recent files in the **File** menu, open it as follows.

Click the **Open** button on the Toolbar.

The Open window appears.

Using Folders

15

The **My Documents** folder is already in the **Look in** box at the top of the window.

Other folders, including the Letters folder you made earlier, appear in the main part of the window underneath.

Double-click the **Letters** folder to open it.

Letters now appears in the **Look in** box and the contents of the folder appear below.

Double-click the **Kathleen** document to open it.

## TIDYING UP

If your **My Documents** folder has a lot of files in it already, use the skills you have learnt in this chapter to organise them and tidy up.

Open the **My Documents** folder and make new folders for different subjects, as described earlier.

Then drag any existing files into their respective folders.

In this chapter, you have learnt...

- how folders are used in a filing cabinet and on your computer in the same way.

- how to display the contents of a folder in different ways.

- how to save a file in a particular folder.

- how to move a file or folder.

Do you remember...

- how to make a new folder?

- how to sort files and folders?

- how to rename files and folders?

- how to re-open a file saved in a particular folder?

Using Folders

15

# CHAPTER 16
# Music and Video

This chapter shows you how to play a music CD or a video DVD on your computer.

Your computer can play a music CD to entertain you and you can carry on working at the computer at the same time. Playing a music CD on your computer is just a matter of inserting the CD. It will normally start playing automatically. If necessary, remember to switch on the loudspeakers.

## INSERTING A CD

Insert a **CD** in the **CD drive** on your computer as follows.

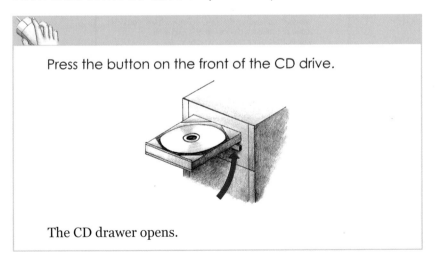

Press the button on the front of the CD drive.

The CD drawer opens.

Music and Video

16

Place the CD in position on the drawer, label side up, shiny side down.

Give the drawer a gentle push to close it. You do not have to push it in all the way.

*Alternatively*, press the button on the front of the drive again to close it (but it is now hidden under the drawer).

After a few moments either the Audio CD window or the Windows Media Player window appears.

## The Audio CD Window

If this is the first time you inserted a music CD, a window appears with **Audio CD** in the title bar. The computer wants to know what you want to do. Notice that **Play Audio CD using Windows Media Player** is already selected.

Click **Always do the selected action** to place a tick in the small box.

This will prevent the window appearing unnecessarily the next time you insert a music CD.

Click **OK** to start playing the CD.

## The Windows Media Player Window

This window appears as the music CD begins to play.

The principal items in the window are described below.

The **tracks** (music) on the CD are listed on the right-hand side, with the track currently playing highlighted.

An animated decorative display – an **Ambiance** – appears in the window while the music is playing.

The main controls are at the bottom of the window on the left.

Music and Video

257

16

## Controls

The controls are in the form of buttons to be clicked and sliders to be dragged. See the illustration below.

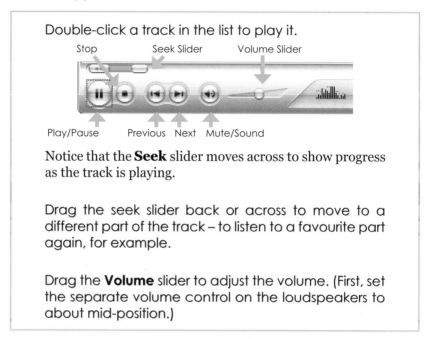

Double-click a track in the list to play it.

Stop    Seek Slider    Volume Slider

Play/Pause    Previous   Next   Mute/Sound

Notice that the **Seek** slider moves across to show progress as the track is playing.

Drag the seek slider back or across to move to a different part of the track – to listen to a favourite part again, for example.

Drag the **Volume** slider to adjust the volume. (First, set the separate volume control on the loudspeakers to about mid-position.)

Just under the **Now Playing** tab at the top of the window are three smaller buttons, should you feel like experimenting. The two right-hand buttons control the Ambiance display, for example.

If you prefer, click the **Minimise** button to hide the window as you listen to the music while you continue to do other work on the computer.

Music and Video

16

## Ejecting and Closing

To eject a CD and close the Windows Media Player, do the following.

Press the **Stop** button in Windows Media Player.

Press the button on the CD drive to open the drawer and eject the CD.

Give the drawer a gentle push to close it when you have removed the CD.

If you minimised the Windows Media Player window earlier, maximise it by clicking the Windows Media Player button on the Taskbar.

Click the small **Close** button in the top right-hand corner to close the Windows Media Player window if you do not want to play another CD.

# Playing a Video DVD

If your computer has a DVD drive, you can watch DVD films on the computer. Check that the computer includes a DVD drive at the time of purchase. A CD drive cannot play DVD disks.

Unlike music CDs, some DVDs use both sides of the disk if necessary – for very long films, for example. A double-sided DVD disk appears to have no label, and you will have to look at the small print around the central hole to know which side is which.

Windows Media Player, described earlier in this chapter, can also play video DVDs.

## INSERTING A DVD

Insert a DVD in the DVD drive on your computer in the same way as you would insert a music CD.

If this is the first time you have inserted a DVD disk, a window similar to the Audio CD window appears, with the name of the DVD in the title bar.

**DVDVolume (E:)** ☒

Windows can perform the same action each time you insert a disk or connect a device with this kind of file:

🔘 DVD movie

What do you want Windows to do?

▶ Play DVD Video
using Windows Media Player

📁 Open folder to view files
using Windows Explorer

🚫 Take no action

☐ Always do the selected action.

OK    Cancel

The computer wants to know what you want to do. Notice that **Play DVD Using Window Media Player** is already selected.

Click **Always do the selected action** to place a tick in the small box.

This will prevent the window appearing unnecessarily every time you insert a DVD disk.

Click **OK** to start playing the DVD.

Music and Video

261

16

## The Windows Media Player Window

This window appears as the DVD begins to play. The principal items in the window have been described under **Playing a Music CD** on page 257.

A menu usually appears in the main part of the window when a DVD is inserted.

Click **Play Movie** to start playing the DVD or click on one of the other menu items as necessary

The scenes on the DVD are usually listed as **Titles** or **Chapters** at the right of the window, with the scene currently playing highlighted.

The main controls are at the bottom of the window, as before.

Notice also the small **Rewind** button (arrowed).

Music and Video

16

## Controls

Use the controls in the same way as you do for an audio CD.

Double-click a scene in the list to play it.
Note that the **Seek** slider moves across to show progress as the scene is playing.

Drag the seek slider back or across to move to a different part of the scene – to watch a favourite part again, for example.

Drag the **Volume** slider to adjust the volume. (First, set the separate volume control on the loudspeakers to about mid-position.)

Click the **Rewind** button to quickly go back. Click the button again to stop and replay.
Notice the two small buttons just above the right-hand corner of the video picture.

Click the left button to view the video at full screen size and hide all the controls.

To return to the previous window size, touch the mouse to reveal the controls again and click the **Exit Full Screen** button in the top right-hand corner of the screen.

Music and Video

16

### Ejecting and Closing

Eject a DVD and close the Windows Media Player as you did for an Audio CD.

Press the **Stop** button in the Windows Media Player (you may need to move the mouse in order for the menu to reappear).

Press the button on the DVD drive to open the drawer and eject the disk.

Give the drawer a gentle push to close it when you have removed the disk.

If you minimised the Windows Media Player window earlier, maximise it by clicking the Windows Media Player button on the taskbar.

Click the small **Close** button in the top right-hand corner to close the Windows Media Player window if you do not want to play another DVD.

In this chapter, you have learnt...

- how to play audio CDs and DVDs on your computer.

- how to set Windows Media Player to play CDs and DVDs.

- how to use the controls in the Windows Media Player window.

Do you remember...

- how to insert and eject a CD or DVD?

- how to play a particular track or scene?

- how to change to and from full screen when playing a DVD?

- how to adjust the volume?

Music and Video

16

# CHAPTER 17

# Buying a Computer

This chapter gives you some advice
and describes what you should look
for when buying a computer.

# Buying a Computer

People buy computers for different reasons. In the business world, computers are bought to do a particular job. Business buyers know what they want the computers to do and they buy ones that are suitable for that particular purpose. The same thing should apply when you buy a computer for personal use or for your home.

Before you rush off to the computer shop, ask yourself why you want to buy a computer. Is it just because 'everyone has one'? Or have you a more specific reason?

Then there is the question of how much you are prepared to spend. This chapter will try to outline the various options that are available and assist you in making your choice.

## MACINTOSH COMPUTERS

There are two main kinds of computer in common use, **Macintosh** and **Windows**. This book deals with the latter, but below is a little information about Macintosh computers.

Macintosh computers – commonly known as **Macs** – are generally regarded as being easier to use but a beginner will probably not see any difference at first.

17

269

Apple iMac computer

Macintosh computers are only made by Apple Computer, in contrast to Windows computers which are made by many different companies under their own brand names.

Apple is famous for innovation and stylish design. It uses its own operating system (see next page), called the **Mac OS,** the software that makes the computer actually work. Popular software, such as **Microsoft Office**, runs on both Macintosh and Windows computers and files and documents can be sent from one to the other.

## WINDOWS COMPUTERS

Windows computers – commonly known as **PCs** – are by far the most common kind of computer. They are widely used in the business world and also in education and by home users.

17

PCs are made by large numbers of different manufacturers. There are many different models available under many different brand names.

Because they are so widely used, there is more software, especially games, available for PCs than for Macintosh computers.

However, depending on what you want to use your computer for, all the most widely used programs, and many of the more popular games, are available for both Macintosh computers and PCs.

## SYSTEM SOFTWARE

Software is the set of programs that makes the computer work.

Without software, the computer is like a car without an engine.

Every computer needs two kinds of software. The first is the **System Software**, which is used by **the computer** to enable it to operate. For this reason it is also known as the **Operating System**. The computer will not work without system software, so when you buy a computer, the system software is always included.

A modern home PC will most likely use **Windows XP Home**, an operating system made by Microsoft Corporation.

Business computers will use **Windows XP Professional** which provides extra facilities suitable for business use.

Older PCs may use earlier versions of **Windows**.

Buying a Computer

17

271

## APPLICATIONS SOFTWARE

The second kind of software is called **Applications Software**. It is used **by you** to do the work you want to do, such as writing letters or playing games, as you have already done with the calculator, Solitaire, word processing, email and the Internet. Without Applications Software, you cannot use your computer to do anything useful. When you buy a home computer, some Applications Software is often included.

Most Windows PCs are often supplied with a suite of programs called **Microsoft Works**.

All Macintosh and Windows PCs for home use are supplied with software for email and Internet access.

Depending on your interests and needs, you may find that extra applications will have to be purchased. **Microsoft Office**, for example, is a widely used suite of applications available for both Macintosh computers and PCs. The cost of extra software can be considerable and should be borne in mind when planning your budget.

## WHAT TO LOOK FOR

There are many things to take into account when you are buying a computer.

### The Processor

The processor is the heart of every computer. It is actually the **Central Processing Unit**, or **CPU**, that gives its name to the **CPU box** described in Chapter 1, page 7.

Buying a Computer

17

Common processors are the **Celeron** and **Pentium** made by Intel, **Athlon** processors made by AMD and **Power PC** processors made by IBM and Motorola.

The speed at which the processor operates is measured in **Gigahertz (GHz)**. As a general rule, the higher the speed, the more efficient (and expensive) the processor. However, processors made by different companies cannot be compared by speed alone, as many other factors are involved. Manufacturers are now beginning to place less emphasis on processor speed.

Processor speeds are now commonly **2.5GHz** or higher.

## Memory

The memory the computer uses is called **RAM** (**R**andom **A**ccess **M**emory), measured in **Megabytes (MB)**. The more memory that is available, the more 'room' the system software has to work in. Extra memory can be added after you have bought your computer but it is better to specify it at the time of purchase, if only to save installation cost and inconvenience.

A computer should have not less than **512MB** of RAM.

## Hard Disk

The hard disk is where the computer's programs and **your work** are stored when the computer is switched off. The storage capacity is measured in **Gigabytes (GB)**. The larger the hard disk, the more storage space you have.

A **40 GB** hard disk may be adequate for many home users but larger hard disks are commonly supplied. If you intend working with graphics, photographs or video, which take up a lot of space, you should consider a hard disk with a larger storage capacity. An additional hard disk can also be added later if necessary.

Buying a Computer

17

### Floppy Disks

A floppy disk drive is no longer supplied as standard with many computers.

If your computer hasn't got a floppy disk drive and you need to use floppy disks, you can specify one to be included at the time of purchase or buy an external unit to plug in to the computer later.

### CD/DVD

Software is commonly distributed on CD, and a CD drive is supplied as standard with all modern computers. It is now common to use recordable CDs for file storage and transfer instead of floppy disks. Note, however, that not all computers are fitted with DVD drives.

Combination (combo) drives – are now common on most computers. As well as being able to use ordinary software and music CDs, they also enable you to save your work for storage or distribution on your own blank CDs. Other combination drives can play DVD disks as well or even enable you to record on blank DVDs.

### Modem

A **56K** modem is used to connect to the Internet and to send email when you have a dial-up connection. Most home computers now have a modem fitted as standard.

If you have a broadband connection, you will need a different kind of modem, usually a separate unit that you connect to the computer.

Buying a Computer

17

## Graphics

Every computer has a graphics facility that is used for the display on the monitor.

If you want to use advanced applications that require a greater graphics capability, a special graphics card can be added to your computer.

## Loudspeakers

Loudspeakers may have to be ordered separately in some cases. They are not always supplied with the computer.

Remember that headphones can be used instead of loud-speakers to prevent disturbance to people around you.

## Monitor

The size of a monitor is measured diagonally across the screen. A **17**" monitor is now the standard for many suppliers. Larger screens – 19" or more – are also available.

A conventional (**CRT**) monitor is usually the heaviest and bulkiest part of a computer, taking up a lot of space on the desk, but they are much cheaper than flat panel screens.

Flat panel (**LCD**) monitors are very compact and take up much less space but they are more expensive. Note that a 15" flat-panel monitor displays the same screen area as a 17" conventional CRT monitor.

## Keyboard and Mouse

A keyboard and mouse are supplied as standard with all computers.

Buying a Computer

17

## Printers and Scanners

A printer is essential if you want to print out your work.

**Inkjet printers** can be very cheap. They use three different coloured inks which are mixed together during printing to produce a full range of colours, as well as a separate black ink.

Cheaper inkjet printers use a single cartridge for the three different colour inks so that when one of the three inks is exhausted, the whole cartridge has to be replaced. More expensive printers use separate cartridges for each colour.

The cost of replacement ink cartridges is very high, perhaps more than you paid originally for the actual printer! Expect to print a few hundred pages from a set of cartridges; less if you use a lot of colour.

Although the cost of the printer may be low, running costs are high. Also, special (expensive) paper is needed to produce high quality colour printouts, which adds further to the running costs.

Note that cheap compatible ink cartridges are available – especially on the Internet – and can save you a lot of money. Claims that third-party cartridges 'may damage your printer' are generally unfounded and contrary to EU policy.

**Laser printers** use toner powder, like photocopiers. They are generally more expensive than inkjet printers but they are much more economical to run. Expect to print several thousand pages before having to replace the toner cartridge. Most laser printers are for black and white printing only but colour laser printers are being more widely used as prices fall.

A **scanner** enables you to put your own artwork, drawings and photographs onto the computer. Note that pictures from a **digital camera** can be transferred directly to the computer without using a scanner.

Buying a Computer

17

## CONNECTING CABLES

Computers are normally supplied with all the necessary cables for their operation.

You should purchase a **4-socket mains extension unit** to connect the various parts of your computer to the mains. You will need to plug in the CPU box, the monitor, the printer and possibly the loudspeakers.

If you have a scanner and a desk lamp as well, a 6-socket extension will be necessary.

A telephone cable to connect your computer to the Internet should also be supplied with the computer.

Printers and scanners require special cables to connect to the computer and some may have to be purchased separately. When purchasing a printer or other device, make sure that you have all the necessary cables.

## MAKING A DECISION

Having read through this chapter, you will know that buying a computer and printer is not perhaps as simple a matter as it may have seemed at first.

First, you should have a clear idea of what the computer is to be used for.

If you only want to do the kind of things you have learnt about in this book, you do not need a very expensive or powerful computer.

Buying a Computer

17

If you want to play the latest computer games with animations and elaborate video effects, then you may need a more powerful computer. And don't forget to budget for the games themselves.

Video enthusiasts who would like to use the computer for editing and for recording their work on DVD may need an even more powerful computer with a faster processor, good video card, lots of memory and a large hard disk.

Be aware that video editing software and associated equipment can be very expensive and will add to the overall cost.

The cheapest computer from a reputable manufacturer will be more than sufficient for basic tasks, such as those outlined in this book.

A modern mid-range computer will do all the things most home users require, including playing games and more demanding tasks.

Only enthusiasts or people with specific requirements should be prepared to spend large sums of money on top-of-the-range computers.

Discuss your requirements with people who have computers already. Each one will have different interests and requirements. Do not depend on just one person's advice. It is better to talk to several people before you make a decision. Then, hopefully, you will buy a computer to suit your own particular requirements and one that will not break the bank.

And will you buy an inkjet printer with its high running costs or a laser printer that will be more expensive, perhaps, but much cheaper to run – or both?

The decisions are yours.

Buying a Computer

17

## In this chapter, you have learnt...

- about Macintosh and Windows computers.

- about system software and applications software.

- about printers and scanners.

- what to look for when buying a computer.

## Do you remember...

- the minimum processor speed you should consider?

- the memory and hard disk sizes you should consider?

- the differences between CRT and flat panel monitors?

- that it is a good idea to discuss your requirements with other people?

Buying a Computer

17

# Appendices

# Appendices

# Screen Resolution

## WHAT IS IT?

Everything that you see on the screen – icons, documents, typing, and so on – is made up of patterns of tiny different coloured dots, or **pixels**. The screen resolution is a measure of the number of pixels that are used.

A **low resolution** screen uses fewer, but larger, pixels.

An object made up of large pixels appears larger on the screen but you may have to use the scroll arrows to see it all.

A **high resolution** screen uses more, but smaller, pixels.

An object made up of small pixels appears smaller on the screen but you can see more of it at a time.

## CHANGING THE SCREEN RESOLUTION

If you would prefer everything to appear a little larger on your computer screen, you can reduce the screen resolution.

Proceed as follows.

**Right-click** anywhere on a blank part of the computer desktop.

Click **Properties** in the menu that appears.

Click the **Settings** tab at the top of the **Display Properties** window that appears.

Arrange Icons By  ▶
Refresh

Paste
Paste Shortcut

New  ▶

Properties

Note the small slider in the **Screen Resolution** area at the bottom left of the window with the current pixel measurements underneath.

**Display Properties**  ? ✕

| Themes | Desktop | Screen Saver | Appearance | Settings |

Display:
Plug and Play Monitor on RADEON FSC

Screen resolution
Less ——————□—— More
1024 by 768 pixels

Color quality
Highest (32 bit)  ▾

Troubleshoot...  Advanced

OK  Cancel  Apply

Drag the slider to the left to give **Less** resolution.

The new resolution appears underneath as you drag the slider.

Click the **Apply** button to apply the resolution you have selected.

The screen goes blank momentarily while the computer resets the screen.

Click **OK** when the screen reappears.

Follow the same steps to restore the original resolution later, but drag the slider to the right instead of to the left.

# Caring for Your Mouse

If the pointer on the screen moves erratically and no longer responds smoothly to the movements of the mouse or you feel a roughness when you move the mouse on its mat, the mouse needs to be cleaned.

Proceed as follows:

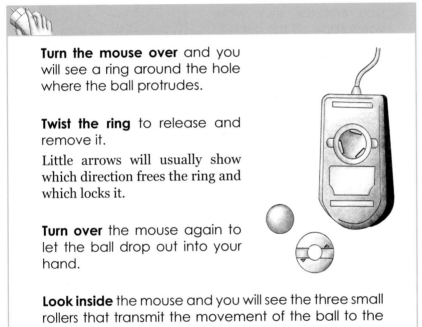

**Turn the mouse over** and you will see a ring around the hole where the ball protrudes.

**Twist the ring** to release and remove it.

Little arrows will usually show which direction frees the ring and which locks it.

**Turn over** the mouse again to let the ball drop out into your hand.

**Look inside** the mouse and you will see the three small rollers that transmit the movement of the ball to the workings of the mouse.

## Cleaning Your Mouse

A dirty mouse will have a little band of dirt around each roller.

Use a small pointed **wooden cocktail stick** to scrape the dirt off the rollers.

Do not use anything metallic or you may scratch and damage the rollers.

The rollers will turn as you try to clean them. This makes it awkward to remove the dirt.

Try to **hold a roller still** with one cocktail stick while you scrape off the dirt with another.

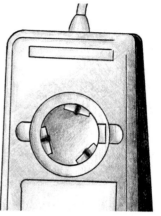

Dirt on the rollers

After cleaning the rollers, use a barely damp soapy cloth to **clean the ball** before you insert it and replace the ring. Ensure the ball is dry before putting it back.

Finally, clean the surface of the **mouse mat**.

Your mouse should now be back to normal.

Optical mice do not get clogged up because there are no moving parts. Nevertheless, they still pick up dust and dirt and should be turned over from time to time and gently cleaned.

And don't forget to clean the mouse mat.

# Mouse – Left Hand

If you operate the mouse with your left hand, you might find it awkward to have to click the left-hand button on the mouse. You can switch over the actions of the buttons if necessary.

Proceed as follows.

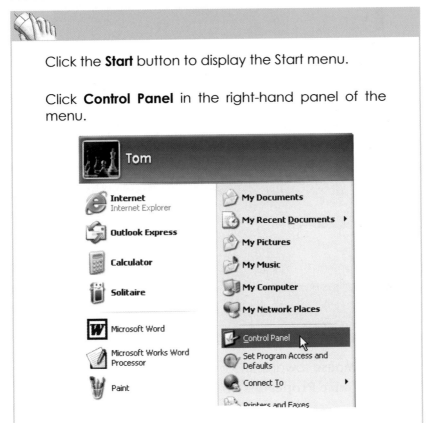

Click the **Start** button to display the Start menu.

Click **Control Panel** in the right-hand panel of the menu.

The control panel window appears.

Click **Printers and other Hardware** towards the top right of the control panel window.

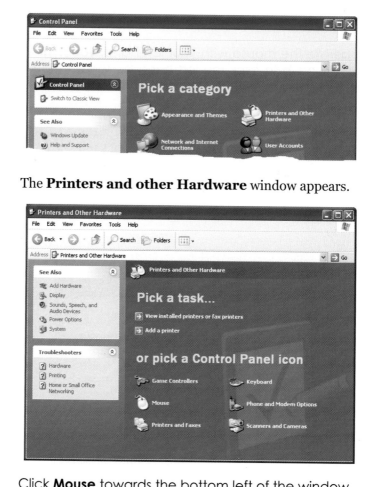

The **Printers and other Hardware** window appears.

Click **Mouse** towards the bottom left of the window.
The **Mouse Properties** window appears.

## The Mouse Properties Window

Follow these steps.

1     Notice that the **left** button of the mouse in the illustration in the window is highlighted.

This shows that the left button is the button used for the most common tasks.

2 Click **Switch primary and secondary buttons** near the top of the window to place a tick in the small box.

Notice that the **right** button on the mouse in the window is now highlighted.

This shows that the **right** button is now the button used for the most common tasks.

3 Now use the **right** mouse button to click the **Apply** button at the bottom of the window to apply the change.

4 Use the **right** mouse button to click the **OK** button at the bottom of the window.

The window closes.

The actions of the two mouse buttons are now set more conveniently for use by a left-handed person.

5 Close the **Printers and Other Hardware** window (click the red **Close** button).

## Remember!

You have switched over the **actions** of the buttons on the mouse.

When you hold the mouse in your left hand, click the **right** button to perform the tasks that were performed by the left button before.

Click the **left** button to perform the tasks that were performed by the right button before.

## Switching Back

Follow the steps as before until the **Mouse Properties** window appears, as in the illustration on page 291. Then continue from Step 2 above.

> Click **Switch primary and secondary buttons** near the top of the window to remove the tick that you place in the small box before.
>
> Now click the **left** button in Steps **3** and **4**.
>
> The mouse buttons have now been restored to their usual actions for right-handed people.

# Deleting Files

## TIDYING UP

The **My Documents** and other folders on your computer will gradually fill up as you store your work in them.

From time to time, however, you may want to discard – or **delete** – old documents or files that you no longer need, if only to tidy up and organise your computer.

## THE RECYCLE BIN

Unwanted files can be placed in the Recycle Bin – the equivalent of the waste paper basket beside an office desk. Like the waste paper basket, the recycle bin has to be emptied from time to time.

Recycle Bin

Files can be deleted in two ways. You can **drag** the file to the recycle bin or you can right-click on a file and click **Delete** in the menu that appears.

### Drag to Delete

First open the folder that contains the file. If the file is in the **My Documents** folder, for example, proceed as follows.

Click the **Start** button to display the Start menu.

Click **My Documents** at the top-right of the Start menu to open the My Documents folder.

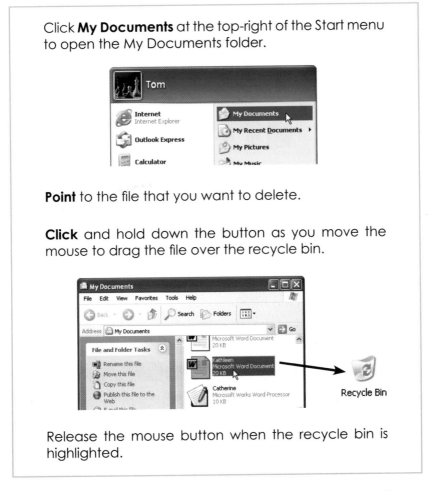

**Point** to the file that you want to delete.

**Click** and hold down the button as you move the mouse to drag the file over the recycle bin.

Release the mouse button when the recycle bin is highlighted.

Dragging a file to the recycle bin is similar to moving a file, as described in Chapter 15, page 246.

## Using the Delete Menu

The computer can place a file in the recycle bin for you, to save you having to drag it there.

Appendices

295

Proceed as follows.

Right-click the file that you want to delete.
A menu appears.

| Open |  |
|------|--|
| New |  |
| Open With | ▶ |
| Send To | ▶ |
| Cut |  |
| Copy |  |
| Create Shortcut |  |
| Delete |  |
| Rename |  |
| Properties |  |

Auburn Villa.wps
Micro
10 KI

Click **Delete** in the menu.

A message window appears asking you to confirm that you want to delete the file.

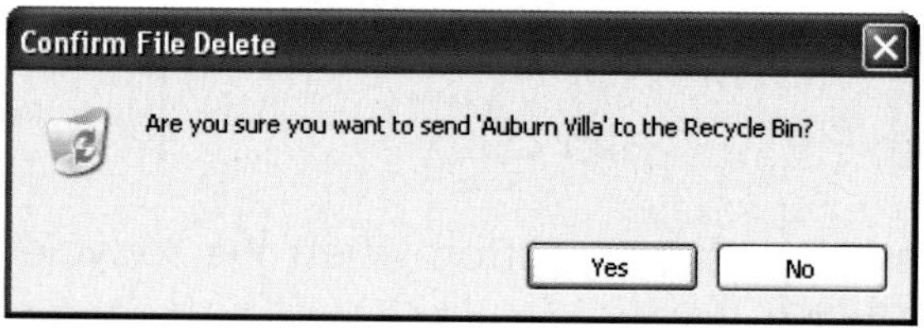

**Confirm File Delete**

Are you sure you want to send 'Auburn Villa' to the Recycle Bin?

Yes     No

Click **Yes**.

The file is placed in the recycle bin and the message window closes.

## Retrieving a Deleted File

Occasionally, you may delete a file and later realise that you still need it. You can retrieve the file provided that you have not emptied the recycle bin **since the file was placed in it**.

Proceed as follows.

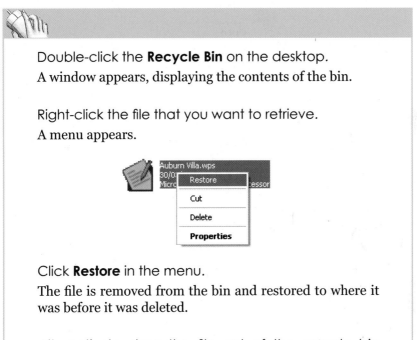

Double-click the **Recycle Bin** on the desktop.
A window appears, displaying the contents of the bin.

Right-click the file that you want to retrieve.
A menu appears.

Click **Restore** in the menu.
The file is removed from the bin and restored to where it was before it was deleted.

*Alternatively*, drag the file out of the recycle bin window and onto the **desktop** or to another location.

## Emptying the Recycle Bin

The files in the recycle bin **remain** there until the bin is emptied, just as paper documents remain in the wastepaper basket under your desk until that is emptied.

To empty the recycle bin, proceed as follows.

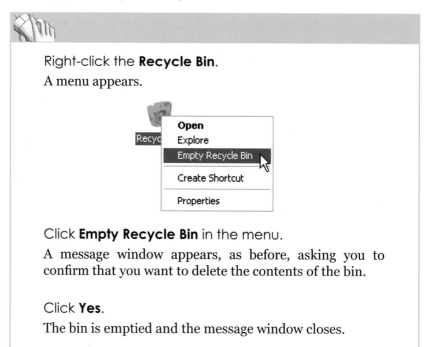

Right-click the **Recycle Bin**.
A menu appears.

Click **Empty Recycle Bin** in the menu.
A message window appears, as before, asking you to confirm that you want to delete the contents of the bin.

Click **Yes**.
The bin is emptied and the message window closes.

# Setting a Home Page

The home page that appears when you open Internet Explorer on a new computer will have been set to reflect the interests of, perhaps, the vendor or computer manufacturer.

This can be changed to suit your own interests, your favourite newspaper or broadcaster, for example.

Here we shall reset the home page that first appears to the home page of Blackrock Education Centre.

First find the page on the Internet that you want to be the home page.

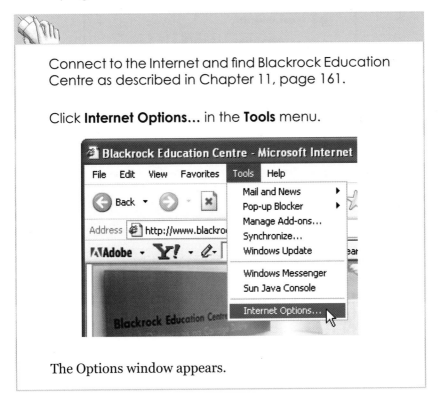

Connect to the Internet and find Blackrock Education Centre as described in Chapter 11, page 161.

Click **Internet Options...** in the **Tools** menu.

The Options window appears.

Click the **Use Current** button in the **Home page** panel near the top of the window.

Note that the **Location** box now contains the new home page address.

Click the **Apply** button at the bottom of the window.

Click the **OK** button to close the window.

The new home page has now been set.

Every time you connect to the Internet again, the home page of Blackrock Education Centre will be the home page that appears.

Try closing Internet Explorer now and then re-opening it to see the new home page appear.

# Your Computer Desk

All of your working time with the computer will be spent sitting in front of it, so you should give a little thought to where it will be situated and how you will work at it.

## HOW WIDE?

You will need a **large** desk or table, not a small one.

At one side of the keyboard will be the mouse on its mouse mat, which should be on the same level as the keyboard. At the other side of the keyboard will be the papers or other documents (perhaps this book!) that you are working with.

You need a desk that is at least **1 metre** wide – a few inches more than 3 feet – to fit everything comfortably.

Appendices

## HOW DEEP?

There must be space behind your desk to allow for cables and to prevent the monitor scraping off the wall. There must be space in front of it for your papers, the keyboard and the mouse mat.

Health and safety regulations require that there must be extra space in front of it so that your face is not up against the monitor, thus causing eye strain.

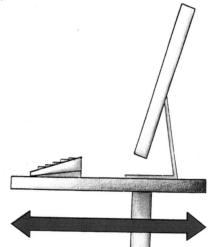

If you are using a bulky CRT monitor, your desk should be at least **80 centimetres** (about 31 inches) deep.

With a flat screen monitor a desk **70 centimetres** (28 inches) or even **60 centimetres** (24 inches) deep may suffice.

# HOW HIGH?

A desk that is too low or high will cause posture and health problems.

A recommended general-purpose height is **75 centimetres** (about 29 inches).

# YOUR CHAIR

What are you going to sit on?

Why not buy a proper office-type chair – even a cheap one – that you can adjust for height and that has a proper back rest?

## Sitting Comfortably

Modern health recommendations state that the **top** of the monitor should **not** be above your eye level.

You should be looking down slightly at the screen, not up, to avoid neck and eye strain.

## THE CPU BOX

The CPU box should be placed on a shelf under the desk, or on the floor beside it.

Placing it on the desktop takes up space needlessly, **even if you have a very large desk**.

## THE PRINTER

If your desk is not large enough, you can place your printer on a small table beside the desk. Printer stands are also available with a shelf underneath for paper and other printer supplies.

## MAINS CABLES

Most computers require a large number of cables to connect everything together. You will typically need mains sockets for the CPU box, monitor, loudspeakers, printer and perhaps a scanner or desk lamp.

Buy a **six-socket mains extension unit**, available from electrical shops, hardware shops and department stores.

## KEEPING CABLES TIDY

Instead of leaving a longer than necessary cable lying around on the floor, you should coil them up and secure them with cable ties.

Cable ties can be bought in electrical supply shops or you can use the ties sold in garden centres for securing flowers and plants.

Appendices

# COMPUTER WORKSTATIONS

A computer workstation is a piece of furniture designed to accommodate your computer, printer, and so on.

Be wary of buying a computer workstation that will prove awkward and inconvenient in use. Many are so narrow that there is not enough space for your papers and the keyboard and perhaps none at all for the mouse and mouse mat. The monitor often has to be placed on a high shelf, a common cause of neck strain.

Appendices

# Computer Workspace Checklist

Before you decide to buy a computer desk or arrange a space on a desk or table at home, here are some questions you should ask yourself.

☐ Is there space for a mouse and mouse mat **beside** the keyboard and on the same level?

☐ Is there a space for my papers beside the keyboard?

☐ Will the keyboard be at a suitable and comfortable height?

☐ Is there enough space for the keyboard in front of the monitor?

☐ Is it deep enough for the monitor to be placed far enough back to avoid eye strain?

☐ Is there a space **under** the desk for my CPU box, or will I have to place it on the floor?

☐ Will I be **looking down** slightly at the monitor and not up?

☐ Is there space for my printer and will I be able insert paper easily?

☐ Is there enough room for my knees and feet?

☐ Will I be able to route all the cables in a neat and tidy fashion?

Appendices

# Your Good Health

## RSI

Actions that you perform over and over again can cause a condition known as **repetitive strain injury**, or **RSI** for short. This is commonly caused by the mouse not being conveniently beside the keyboard or not being on the same level. You may feel a pain in your wrist or a knotted muscle and a sharp stabbing sensation in the shoulder-blade area.

## WRIST AND NECK STRAIN

Strain in the wrists can occur if the keyboard is not at the correct level. Muscle strain is also caused at the back of the neck if the monitor is too high and you have to work with your head tilted back all the time. You will recognise neck strain as an ache or stabbing sensation in the back of the neck.

## EYE STRAIN

Eye strain can occur if you are too close to the monitor, having to focus continually on what you are doing. If your desk is not deep enough to push the monitor back, get a deeper desk.

Place your monitor where direct sunlight does not fall on it, as this will make it difficult to see what is on the screen. Avoid placing the monitor where a window will be reflected on the screen, for the same reason.

Appendices

# RADIATION

Modern CRT monitors (the big and heavy ones) have to comply with strict health and safety regulations regarding radiation. It should not be necessary to use any of the special 'anti-radiation' or other filters commonly sold in computer shops.

Flat-screen monitors operate on a different principle and do not emit any radiation at all.

# BREAKS

Even when you are careful and your computer is correctly placed and set up, long periods of work at it without a rest are not a good idea. You should take regular breaks, get up and walk around for 10 minutes every hour.

Be sensible… and enjoy your computer.

Glossary

| | |
|---|---|
| Apple | Computer company that manufactures Macintosh computers and other equipment. |
| applications software | The programs used by the computer user to do his or her work. |
| arrow keys | A set of four keys on the keyboard used to move up or down, left or right, in a word processing document, for example. |
| attachment | A document or other file that is sent with an email message. |
| bar | A narrow strip, usually across the top of a window, that contains buttons or menus. |
| broadband | A method of connecting to the Internet that is considerably faster that a dial-up connection in use and that requires no dial-up or disconnection procedure. |
| browser | An Internet browser enables you to view pages on the Internet. Other browsers may be used to view collections of photographs, etc. |
| button | (On the screen) a small area that can be clicked with the mouse to tell the computer to perform an action. A button usually has an icon or text on it to indicate its purpose. |
| CD | Compact Disk. The standard format for storing recorded music (audio CD) and computer files (CD-ROM). |
| CD drive | A unit for using CD disks in a computer. |
| chips | Small electronic blocks – on a computer motherboard, for example — that perform certain functions. |

**Glossary**

313

| | |
|---|---|
| clicking | Pressing a button on the mouse momentarily to send an instruction to the computer. |
| code | Text and symbols used to send instructions to a computer. |
| computer | A multi-purpose electronic machine now commonly used in business and industry, education and individual homes. |
| CPU | Central Processing Unit. The part of a computer that processes information and thus performs the actions required by the user. Also used to describe the box in which the CPU and other parts of a computer are contained. |
| crosshair | A pointer used for accurate positioning on the screen. |
| CRT | Cathode Ray Tube. Large, heavy display units used in many monitors and television sets. |
| cursor | See pointer. |
| desktop | The screen that appears on the monitor when the computer has finished starting up. |
| dial-up | A method of connecting to the Internet where the computer actually dials a telephone number to make the connection. |
| digital camera | A camera that records pictures as computer data instead of using film. |
| dragging | Using the mouse to move an object from one part of the screen to another. |

Glossary

| | |
|---|---|
| DVD | Digital Versatile Disk. Device that is able to store considerably more data than CDs. The standard for video and films, replacing VHS tape cassettes. |
| DVD drive | A unit for using DVD disks in a computer. |
| email address | An address, unique to each user, used for sending and receiving email. |
| email | A method of sending and receiving messages electronically over the Internet. |
| file | Any document, picture or other data that can be stored on a computer. |
| floppy disk | A portable soft plastic magnetic disk principally used to transfer files between one computer and another. Now superseded by CDs and other media which have a much larger storage capacity. |
| floppy disk drive | A unit for using floppy disks in a computer. |
| folder | A container for a number of documents or other files, shown on the screen by an icon resembling a paper folder. |
| font | The set of letters and symbols in a particular type and style. Different fonts, such as Times New Roman and Arial, display the same characters differently. |
| hard disk | A magnetic device on which computer data is stored. |
| home page | The first page on a website. Also used to describe the page displayed by an Internet browser when it first opens. |

Glossary

| | |
|---|---|
| icon | A small picture or symbol with an easily understood meaning, used instead of text and thus independent of language. |
| inbox | The folder in which received email is stored. The inbox is normally displayed by default when an email program is used. |
| inkjet printer | A printer that uses a fine spray of ink to print on paper or other media. |
| insertion point | In word processing, a flashing cursor that shows where text will appear when typed. |
| Internet | A worldwide network of computers, of which the world wide web is an important part, that enables information to be shared and viewed. |
| ISP | Internet Service Provider. A company that provides its customers with access to the Internet. |
| laser printer | A printer that uses a laser to direct fine powder onto paper or other media where it is then sealed on by heat. |
| LCD | Liquid Crystal Display. A display technique used in flat-panel computer monitors and television sets, enabling much thinner and lighter units to be made. |
| link | A piece of text, button or graphic on an Internet page that, when clicked, displays a related page. |
| keyboard | A device for entering information in a computer by typing, similar to a typewriter keyboard but usually with many extra keys. |

Glossary

| | |
|---|---|
| laptop | Generic name for small, portable computers. |
| Macintosh | Brand of computer made by Apple Computers, named after a variety of apple grown in California. |
| malware | A term for malicious programs, commonly spread via email and the Internet, that can cause problems on you computer. |
| maximise | Increase the size of a window to fill the screen. |
| memory | Electronic chips used to store data temporarily only while the computer is switched on. Not to be confused with the hard disk, which is used for permanent storage. |
| menu | A list of items from which a choice can be made by clicking. |
| Microsoft | A company that produces and markets operating systems and other computer software. |
| minimise | Temporarily remove a window from the desktop to become a button on the taskbar. |
| modem | A device used to connect to the Internet when a dial-up connection is used. |
| monitor | The screen used to display information for the user. |
| motherboard | The principal electronic circuit board of a computer. |

Glossary

| | |
|---|---|
| mouse | A small hand-held device used to send instructions to a computer. |
| mouse mat | A small mat on which the mouse is placed to facilitate its use. |
| password | A number of characters and/or numbers used as to prevent unauthorised access. |
| PC | Personal Computer. Generic name for modern desktop computers. |
| pixel | Contraction of picture element. One of the dots that make up an image on the screen. See also screen resolution. |
| pointer | A small arrow, that moves around on the screen in response to the movement of the mouse or the pressing of keys on the keyboard. |
| pointing | Moving the mouse so that the pointer rests on an object on the screen. |
| power supply | The unit, usually in the CPU box, that converts the mains electricity supply to a form usable by the computer. |
| processor | See CPU. |
| program | A computer application, such as a word processor, used for a specific purpose. |
| RAM | Random Access Memory. See memory. |
| recycle bin | The screen equivalent of a wastepaper basket in which unwanted files can be placed before being permanently discarded. |

**Glossary**

| | |
|---|---|
| resolution | See screen resolution. |
| return key | A large key on the right of the keyboard used for many purposes – to create a new paragraph in a word processing application, for example. |
| saving | The act of storing a file on a computer so that it can be used later. |
| search engine | A website that searches for information on the Internet and displays the results of the search as a series of links. |
| scanner | A unit for copying pictures or other graphic material onto a computer. |
| screen resolution | A measure of the number of pixels that are used to display the screen on the monitor. Large pixels make an object appear larger but 'chunkier'; smaller pixels make it appear smaller but sharper. |
| scroll arrows | Small buttons at the ends of a scroll bar. Clicking or holding down the mouse button on a scroll arrow moves the page on the screen. |
| scroll bar | A bar that appears at the side or bottom of the screen in some applications. A slider on the bar can be dragged to move the page more quickly that by using the scroll arrows. |
| spyware | Programs, commonly spread via email and the Internet, that can send information from you computer to a remote site without your knowledge. |
| Start button | A button at the left of the taskbar used to access many of the computer's programs, etc. |

Glossary

| | |
|---|---|
| system software | The programs used by the computer to operate, and largely invisible to the user. |
| taskbar | A bar along the bottom of the desktop used to display common or frequently used items. |
| username | A (usually short) name – to identify a customer to an ISP, for example. |
| virus | A malicious program, commonly spread via email and the Internet, that can cause serious problems on you computer. |
| web address | An address that uniquely identifies every page on the Internet. |
| web mail | An email system that uses an Internet browser instead of an email program. |
| website | A collection of pages published by companies or individuals on the Internet. |
| Windows | A system developed by Microsoft Corporation to display commonly used computer actions in graphical form on the computer screen. |
| Windows XP | A Microsoft Corporation operating system used on modern computers. |
| world wide web | The part of the Internet used by most people when they are using 'the Internet'. |

Glossary

Index

Index

Index

Index

# Notes

Notes

# Notes

# Notes

# Notes